PREFACE

This series now seems well established. We hope that ....
will usefully extend the range of the series by providing translations of literary
sources which throw light upon the development of the democracy at Athens, mainly
in the second half of the fifth century B.C. - a theme which is central to any study
of Athens in this period.

This volume might never have seen the light of day were it not for a new
arrangement by which the Classical Association now joins with the London Association of the Classical Teachers in promoting this venture. The translations are the
work of a dozen or more teachers, some of them members of the LACT Ancient
History Group, others of the JACT Ancient History Bureau, for whose cooperation
we are most grateful .

We have been very fortunate in being able to base this selection of literary
sources very closely upon that in 'From Pericles to Cleophon', edited by M.S. Warman,
I. Sutherland and C. Macdonald, published by Rivingtons in 1954. The Greek
texts which are given there are supplemented by valuable notes and indices, and
although our translations, glossary and index should stand on their own, there
may be many who will benefit from using this volume in conjunction with the
original 'From Pericles to Cleophon'. The only variations from the selection
presented there are as follows:-

We have omitted Antiphon, On the Murder of Herodes 76-80, and On the
Choreutes 15 and 33-45; and Plato, Apology 36 B - 38 B, and Laws 704 A - 707 C:
and have inserted Herodotus 5.66-67 and 69; the Anonymous Drinking-song on
Harmodius and Aristogeiton; one fragment each from Cratinus and Eupolis;
Euripides, Medea 824-845; Plato, Republic 488 A-E, and Crito 50 C - 53 A;
and Thucydides 5.84-114, 115.4, and 116.2-4.

For reasons of space, however, we have not included translations of
Thucydides, but by giving references both to the original Greek text and to the
page-numbers of the Penguin translation of Thucydides, we hope that readers will
be encouraged to look up the passages of Thucydides in their relevant context.
Likewise, for the old Oligarch reference is made to LACTOR 2.

Brief introductory notes are given to many of the passages, and information
about each author is regularly given on that author's first appearance. These
sections are indented to distinguish them from the translations that follow. The
Glossary gives further information about significant words which have been underlined in the main text. Since these terms fall naturally into groups according to subject
matter, they are not presented in alphabetical order in the Glossary, but the reader
should avoid any difficulty on this account by reading through the Glossary before em-
barking on the main text. The Index, which is in alphabetical order, gives references to a
wider range of words, covering not only the translations in this volume, but also the
passages from Thucydides and the Old Oligarch to which reference is made.

We owe a great debt of gratitude to Mr M.S. Warman for his valuable help in
preparing the Glossary and the Index and for checking our translations and making
helpful suggestions for improvements. He is of course in no way responsible for
any inaccuracies that may remain. We are also most grateful to Rivingtons Ltd.
for kindly allowing us to follow 'From Pericles to Cleophon' so closely; to the
Clarendon Press for permission to base our translations on the Oxford Classical
Texts of Aristophanes, Herodotus, Euripides, Xenophon, Lysias, Plato, Demosthenes and Aristotle's Constitution of Athens, and on the texts of Cratinus and Eupolis
and the Drinking-song on Harmodius and Aristogeiton in the Oxford Book of Greek
Verse, and on the text of Hermippus printed in Greek Comic Fragments, edited by Sir
A.W. Pickard-Cambridge; to Messrs B.G. Teubner for permission to follow their texts
of Antiphon, Andocides, Isocrates, Plutarch and Aristotle's Politics; and to the Loeb
Classical Library for permission to follow their text of Minor Attic Orators I, pp. 294-296.

Editor:- R.W.J. CLAYTON,   The LACT Ancient History Group.
         East Ham G.S. for Boys,
         London, E.6.

i

TABLE OF CONTENTS

ALPHABETICAL LIST OF AUTHORS

(Thucydides is not included in this alphabetical list).

NOTES, ABBREVIATIONS etc.

All dates are B.C. unless otherwise stated.

All numbers on the left-hand side of the page refer to the line- or section-numbers of the Greek text. Page numbers are given at the bottom, and Chapter numbers at the top right, of each page.

Further information about words which are underlined in the text will be found in the Glossary, but such words are not underlined on any subsequent occurrence within the same passage. There are also a few Greek words which have been placed in brackets beside their translation, but are not underlined or given in the Glossary. Other bracketed words are editorial additions intended to clarify the meaning of the passage, and are not translations of the Greek text.

OBGV - Oxford Book of Greek Verse.

P. - e.g. See Thucydides 1.70.2-9 (P.51) - see page 51 of the Penguin translation of Thucydides by Rex Warner (1954).

GLOSSARY

N.B. For significant passages relating to the more important of these terms,
see the Index.

1. The following are neutral terms applied to features of Athenian political organisation.
By 'neutral terms' is meant terms which do not normally carry with them any tone
of praise or blame.

DĒMOS and PLĒTHOS - These words have a similar range of political meaning.
They may mean, according to context
1) The common people (as opposed to the aristocracy, the rich, etc.)
2) The whole citizen body
3) Democracy
4) The popular assembly.
Plēthos, (like HOI POLLOI - the multitude) has the basic sense of 'the great
number' or 'the mass'.
Dēmos has the additional meaning of 'deme', or 'parish'. The mayor, or
president of a deme, was called a DĒMARCH.

Assembly   (ekklēsia) - The popular Assembly, usually held on the PNYX, a slope near
the Acropolis and above the AGORA, the market place.   (For the functions
of the Assembly and the meaning of KURIA EKKLĒSIA, see p. 9).

Council   (boulē) - The Council of 500, which prepared business for the Assembly and
acted on its behalf.   (For its composition and functions, see p. 9).

PRYTANEIS - The presiding sub-committee of the Council, 50 in number, provided by
each tribe in turn. (See p. 9).

EPISTATĒS   - The chairman of the prytaneis.

PRYTANY - The period (35 or 36 days) during which each board of prytaneis held office.

PRYTANEION - The Town Hall, where outstanding citizens (e.g. victors in the pan-
Hellenic games, or distinguished generals) were entertained for life at
public expense.   (N.B. PRYTANEIA were court-fees paid by both parties
before a lawsuit began).

THOLOS - The Rotunda in which the prytaneis fed and slept.

ARCHERS (toxotai) - used by the prytaneis as disciplinary officers to control meetings
of the Council or Assembly.

CRIER   (kērux) - made announcements in the Assembly and called for speakers.

RHĒTORES - Those people who made a habit of speaking in the Assembly.

PROSTATĒS TOU DĒMOU - Whatever rhētor was for the time being regarded by the
dēmos (in sense 1) as best representing its interests; an entirely unofficial
position.   Similar is DĒMAGŌGOS, leader of the demos (in sense 1), but
it came to be used almost always in a derogatory sense.

PROBOULEUMA - A motion drafted by the Council for the Assembly to discuss and
vote upon.

PSĒPHISMA - A decree of the Assembly.

GRAPHĒ PARANOMŌN - An indictment against a decree or the proposer of a decree
that was alleged to conflict with a law or to have been passed unconstitutionally.

EISANGELIA - Prosecution before the Council or the Assembly.

EUTHŪNAI - A public scrutiny of an official's conduct, held at the end of his term.
HYPEUTHŪNOS - liable to such scrutiny.
ANEUTHŪNOS, ANHYPEUTHŪNOS - not liable to such scrutiny.

DOKIMASIA - A public scrutiny of qualifications (for office, citizenship, etc.).

POLITEIA   - A word of many meanings, according to context: they include
1) Citizenship, 2) Policy, 3) Government, 4) Constitution. (In sense 4,
only the English translation is given, without the Greek word being added).

STASIS -   A faction or a state of faction in the city.

GENERALS (stratēgoi) - Military officers, 10 in number, with important political powers.
(See p. 10).

ARCHONS - The 9 officials whose main duty was to preside in the courts.

THESMOTHETAI - The 6 junior archons (i.e. not the Eponymous, King or Polemarch).

AUTOKRATŌR - An official (e.g. a General) described as 'autokrator' had plenipotentiary
powers 'ad hoc' and could take decisions without reference to the Assembly;
this did not exempt him from euthūnai at the end of his term.

PROBOULOI - An emergency committee of 10 for legislative purposes, set up soon after
the Sicilian disaster of 413.

HELIAEA - The chief and largest of the lawcourts.

KŌLAKRETĒS - The Treasurer responsible for payment to jurymen. The phrase
'Treasurer's milk' refers to this pay.

BAR (kinklis or drŭphaktoi) - The railings of the Council-chamber or the lawcourts
which separated the place where the Councillors or jurymen sat from the
space 'below the bar'. No unauthorised person should pass within the bar.

AREOPAGUS - The Council of the Areopagus, consisting of former archons. Membership
was for life. It was important mainly as the court where cases of murder
were tried.

ODEION - A public building built by Pericles for musical performances, but commonly
used as a lawcourt.

ADEIA - An immunity or amnesty granted by the Assembly or the Council, either
1) to women, metics and slaves, as special permission to speak before the
meeting granting it, or
2) to criminals who volunteered information.

ATĪMIA - Disfranchisement, either total or partial loss of civil rights. (See p. 38f).
Those who were fully enfranchised were said to be ENTIMOI or EPITĪMOI.
There was an intermediate stage of citizenship to which the PLATAEANS
were admitted; they could not hold an archonship or take part in certain
religious ceremonies, but were otherwise full citizens.

ELEVEN - The eleven commissioners of police.

LITURGY (leitourgia) - A public service expected of the rich. (See p.50ff).

HOPLITES - Heavy-armed infantry. Since they were expected to provide their own
armour, the term is used of the richest class of citizen.

THĒTES - The poorest class of citizen.

METIC - A resident alien, settled in Athens.

2. The following are political terms which usually indicate a degree of bias on the part
of the user. The bias is usually anti-democratic. (On the political use of moral
terms where it is at its most rampant, see The Old Oligarch, introduction and text,
in LACTOR 2).

SYCOPHANT - Originally simply a voluntary denouncer of an alleged criminal. In the
absence of a public prosecutor, the operation of justice depended on such
volunteers. But the excessive number of enthusiastic volunteers (especially
to denounce the rich) brought the word into disrepute and 'sycophantein' came
to be almost synonymous with 'diaballein', with nuances of both slander and
blackmail. (See p. 27f).

NEŌTERIZEIN - 'To introduce new ideas', but usually with the implication that new
ideas are bad or revolutionary ideas. (Cf. 'novae res').

OCHLOS and HOMILOS - 'Rabble' and 'mob' are terms used of the plēthos by those who
disapproved of it. Similar, but much rarer, is KOLOSYRTOS.

HETAIREIA - Originally 'an association of friends', but it was especially used of
political clubs with oligarchic intentions. Members of these clubs were
amongst those who were suspected, particularly by demagogues, of being
SYNOMOTAI (conspirators) against democracy.

A variety of terms was used to describe those who stood apart from the plēthos and
were usually (though not necessarily) hostile to it:-

AMEINONES or BELTIONES - 'the better men'.

ARISTOI or BELTISTOI - 'the best men'.

DUNATOI, DUNAMENOI or DUNASTEUONTES - 'the men of influence and
ability'.

EPIEIKEIS - 'the moderate men'.

EPIPHANEIS - 'the men of distinction'.

EUGENEIS or GENNAIOI - 'the men of nobility'.

GNORIMOI or DOKIMOI - 'the men of note'.

KALOI K'AGATHOI - 'the men of good breeding', 'true gentlemen'.

SŌPHRONES - 'the sensible men'.

CHRĒSTOI - 'the sound, respectable men'.

The characteristic virtue ascribed to all these was SŌPHROSYNĒ, (moderation,
good sense, restraint).

Men who were regarded as neither well-born nor well-bred nor reasonable nor sound were
nearly always called PONĒROI. Akin to ponēros is MOCHTHĒROS; also
AGENNĒS (low-born) and BANAUSOS (a mechanic or worker in a vulgar
trade). The particular bad qualities attached to the ponēroi are:- AKOLASIA

(lack of self-control), AMATHIA and APAIDEUSIA (lack of education),
POLYPRAGMOSYNĒ (meddlesomeness). APRAGMOSYNĒ (refraining
from officious political activity) is usually a complimentary term.

DRONE-bee - The metaphor of the drone was used to symbolise those citizens who
contributed nothing, but lived off their more useful fellows.

EUNOMIA - 'A state of good law' usually implies not only that the laws are good but
that they are obeyed, and has the same overtones as our word 'discipline'. It
represented part of the ideal of 'the men with the CAULIFLOWER EARS'
(p. 15), i.e. those in Athens who admired Sparta.

ISONOMIA - 'A state of equality under the law' expresses the contrasting democratic
ideal. The other words which appealed to democratic emotions were:-
'Freedom' and 'equality' (which are simply translated thus in the text, without
their Greek equivalents 'eleutheria' and 'isotēs' being given), ISĒGORIA and
PARRHĒSIA (freedom of speech). EXOUSIA (permissiveness) and PRAOTĒS
(leniency) were aspects of the democratic ideal which came in for criticism
from opponents.

3. Some Greek words (without special political significance) which have no exact
equivalent in English.

a) Financial. 6 OBOLS - 1 DRACHMA
100 DRACHMAE - 1 MINA (mna)
60 MINAE - 1 TALENT

In the time of Aristophanes, a STATER was equal to 4 drachmae.
It is not possible to give exact English equivalents. 3 obols a day seems to
have been something like a minimum wage between 430 - 400.

DIŌBELIA - A payment of 2 obols a day. It is uncertain whether it was paid to the
needy as a war emergency measure, or, more likely, for any kind of service
to the state. Introduced after the overthrow of the Four Hundred in 410, it
was repealed by the Thirty, but restored after their overthrow.

b) HUBRIS - The sort of arrogance which leads a man to ignore the restraints of religion
or his fellow-men and leads to violent, unscrupulous behaviour. It was
particularly associated with tyrants.

ARETĒ - Excellence of any kind; the capacity of a creature or thing to perform that
for which it was intended. It is particularly used of moral excellence in
general or of courage in particular.

SOPHIA - covers a range of meanings between wisdom and intelligence.

TECHNĒ - covers a range of meanings between skill and art.

GYMNASTIKĒ and MOUSIKĒ were the two parts of basic education (PAIDEIA),
gymnastikē meaning physical training and mousikē meaning intellectual(and
moral) training through music and poetry. AMOUSOS means uncultured.

c) Festivals.

PANATHENAEA - celebrated each year early in August, and with special magnificence
(the Great Panathenaea) every fourth year. It lasted 6 to 9 days and included
athletic and musical contests and a ceremonial offering of a peplos (robe) to
Athena.

DIONYSIA - The Great or City Dionysia, at the end of March, was the main annual
dramatic festival, when most new tragedies and many new comedies were
produced. Also held in honour of Dionysus were the Country or Rustic
Dionysia, in December; and the Lenaea, at the end of January, when many
new comedies were produced.

APATURIA - This festival lasted 3 days early in November and was held to celebrate
new enrolments into the PHRATRIES (each tribe was composed of 3 phratries);
it signified the religious recognition of citizenship.

THARGĒLIA - held late in May in honour of Apollo; singing contests took place
between choruses, both men's and boys'.

PLYNTĒRIA - held early in June, at which the clothes of Athena's statue were washed.

PROMĒTHEA - Torch-race contests were held at this festival in honour of Prometheus.

DIPOLIEIA - An ancient festival of Zeus, held in the far-distant days when the
Athenians wore gold cicadas in their hair. One of its ceremonies was the
Bouphonia, the sacrifice of oxen.

1. THE ATHENIAN CHARACTER BEFORE THE PELOPONNESIAN WAR

See Thucydides 1. 70. 2-9 (P. 51).

> For other comments on the Athenian character, cf. Thucydides 6. 18.
> (P. 378-380); 3. 38. (P. 181-182); 2. 62-63. (P. 131-132); and
> Xenophon, Memorabilia 3. 5. 15-17, p .44.

> For Thucydides' statement about his method in composing his speeches,
> see Thucydides 1. 22. 1. (P. 24).

2. CHARACTERISTICS OF DEMOCRACY

> HERODOTUS lived and wrote (largely at Athens) in the heyday of Periclean
> democracy; he may have lived long enough to know of the death of Pericles
> and of Cleon's rise to power. He made the following comments when
> writing about two battles won by the Athenians on the same day in 506 soon
> after the expulsion of Hippias (510).

Herodotus 5. 78.

78   It is clear in every possible way how fine a thing is freedom of speech (isēgoria),
because when governed by tyrants the Athenians were no better in war than any of
their neighbours, but when freed from tyrants they were by far the best. So it is
clear that when held down they deliberately fought shy, as working for a master,
but when they were freed each one of them was eager to labour for his own advantage.

Harmodius and Aristogeiton

> These young men who killed Hipparchus in 514 became symbols of 'freedom
> under the law' (isonomia) to those Athenians who opposed both tyrants and
> aristocrats. Cf. Herodotus 5. 55 and Thucydides 6. 54-59. 1.(P. 399-402).

Anonymous Drinking-song. OBGV No. 230.

In a myrtle spray will I carry my sword, as did Harmodius and Aristogeiton when
5   they slew the tyrant and made Athens the land of equal rights (isonomos). Dearest
Harmodius, you cannot surely be dead, but men say you dwell in the islands of the
blessed where dwells swift-footed Achilles and, so they say, noble Diomede, son of
10   Tydeus. In a myrtle spray will I carry my sword, as did Harmodius and Aristogeiton,
when at Athena's festival they slew the tyrant Hipparchus. For ever will your fame
15   endure upon the earth, dearest Harmodius and Aristogeiton, because you slew the
tyrant and made Athens the land of equal rights (isonomos).

Herodotus on types of Government

> In a longer passage, purporting to contain a debate between the leading
> Persians after the death of Cambyses, Herodotus makes one of the first
> contributions to Greek political philosophy.

Herodotus 3. 80-82. 4.

80. 1 After the turmoil died down and the fifth day had passed, those who were rebelling
against the Magi discussed the situation and made the following speeches; they may
2   seem incredible to some of the Greeks, but nonetheless they were made. Otanes
wanted to entrust the government to the whole Persian nation. 'I think', he said,
'that we must not have one of our number as a king. This is neither pleasant nor
profitable. You have seen how far the pride (hubris) of Cambyses went, and you
3   have borne your part of the hubris of the Magus. How can a monarchy be a balanced
affair, if the ruler can do whatever he likes without being called to account
(aneuthūnos)? If you gave this power to the best (aristos) man on earth, he would
be corrupted by it. The advantages of his present position breed hubris in him, and
4   envy is a natural instinct in man. The two combine to make him altogether evil.
For in his state of satiation he will do many wicked things, some from envy, some
from hubris. A tyrant ought to be the least envious of all men, since he has
everything. But of course, it is the very opposite of this that occurs in his dealings
with his citizens. He is envious of the continued safety of the best men (aristoi), and
5   rejoices at the survival of the evil. No man is more apt to believe slander. He is

the hardest of all men to please. If you give him only such honour as is his due,
he is annoyed that you do not worship him to excess, but if you do so, he damns
you for being obsequious. And there is worse. He overturns the law of the land,
6 he rapes the women and puts men to death without trial. Whereas if the plēthos
rule, their virtue lies first in the fair name of isonomia, and second in the fact
that they commit none of the sins of a single ruler. All offices are assigned by
lot, and their power is subject to scrutiny (hypeuthūnos), and all plans are publicly
debated. So I declare my opinion that we should lay aside monarchy and give more
power to the plēthos. For all good lies with the majority'.

81.1 These were Otanes' suggestions. Megabyzus however was for an oligarchy, saying :
'I agree with all that Otanes has said against tyranny, but he has not hit upon the
best (aristos) policy when he suggests a democracy. Nothing shows less sense or
2 more hubris than the useless mob (homilos). It is intolerable that in trying to
escape from the hubris of a tyrant, we should exchange it for the hubris of the
uncontrolled (akolastos) dēmos. For whatever a tyrant does, at least he acts
with knowledge, but the people cannot even do this. What knowledge could they
have when they have neither been educated nor seen anything lovely (kalon) in their
home surroundings? They fall headlong into things and rush at them like a river
3 in spate. Let those who would bring harm to Persia adopt a democracy, but let
us choose a number of the best (aristoi) men and put them in power. I include
ourselves, of course. Where you have the best (aristoi) men, there it is likely
you will have the best (aristos) counsel'.

82.1 That was Megabyzus' suggestion. Darius was third to speak. 'Megabyzus', he
said, 'was quite right about democracy, but not about oligarchy. For if this is
where the choice lies, among the best (aristoi) specimens of all three, I say that
2 monarchy is far superior. Nothing seems to me better than the rule of one really
good (aristos) man; if his judgement is as good as he is, he will rule the plēthos
faultlessly, and will be the best at concealing his plans for the destruction
3 of his enemies. In an oligarchy, where all wish to serve the state with distinction,
private feuds are likely to flourish; for each one wants to be at the top, so that
his counsels may prevail. And so they come to hate each other bitterly. Enmity
breeds faction (stasis) and stasis breeds bloodshed, and out of it all a monarchy
4 results, - showing that this is the best (aristos) in the first place. Again, the rule
of the dēmos necessarily brings about corruption, and when corruption occurs, this
leads not to mutual hostility between the wrongdoers, but to firm alliances. For
those who wish the state ill begin to act in secret concert. This continues until
someone becomes prostatēs tou dēmou, and puts a stop to this corruption. He
therefore becomes the idol of the dēmos, and being their idol is made their monarch,
- which also shows that monarchy is the best!'

Democracy and Tyranny - a Stage Argument

> This passage by the Athenian tragedian EURIPIDES (c. 480 - 406) is a conspicu-
> ous example of the political argument to be found in many of his plays and
> shows the influence of the sophists on his style. The Suppliants was written
> in the latter half of the Archidamian War.

Euripides, Suppliants 399-441; 476-493

Herald:- Who is tyrant of this land? To whom should I address the message
400 sent by Creon, who has been lord of Cadmus' land since Eteocles was killed by his
brother's hand before the sevenfold gates (of Thebes)?
Theseus:- Firstly, you begin your speech on a false note, stranger, by asking for
405 a tyrant here. For this city is free and not ruled by one man. It is the dēmos
that rules as year by year new men succeed to office, giving no advantage to the
rich, while even the poor have equal rights.
410 Herald:- Admitting this to me is like giving me the first throw at dice. For
I come from a city ruled by one man, , not by the rabble (ochlos). There is no
one there to puff up the city with speeches and to twist men's wavering minds for
415 private gain - popular for a moment and conferring great favours, but later bringing
harm upon the city, then making further wild accusations so as to disguise his
former mistakes and escape justice. Besides, how could the dēmos guide a city
rightly if they cannot even talk straight? For it is time, not haste, that gives men better
420 instruction (mathēsis). The poor man who tills the land, even if he does not suffer

from lack of education (<u>amathia</u>) would not be able to attend exclusively to the
public good, because of his own work. Indeed, it causes resentment among the
425 better men (<u>ameinones</u>) when a jumped-up commoner (<u>poneros</u>) gets respect
because his tongue gains him a hold on the dēmos.
Theseus:- Yes, the herald is smart and quite a master of words. But since
you have entered upon this contest, listen to me. For it was you who gave the
challenge for a debate. A city has no worse enemy than a tyrant: for under a
430 tyrant, above all, the laws do not belong to the community, but one man takes
possession of them and he governs on his own. And so equality is lost. But
with written laws both the weak and the rich have equal rights and it is possible
435 for the weaker man, if insulted, to reprove the prosperous in the same terms,
and an inferior, if his cause is just, can overcome the powerful. This is the
call that freedom makes:- 'Who has good (<u>chrēstos</u>) counsel for the city and
440 wishes to propose it publicly?' The man who does this gains glory, whereas he
who does not, keeps silent. How can there be greater equality than this in a city?

> The Herald eventually dismisses ideologies and reflects on the over-
> riding folly of war.

476 Herald:- Reflect, and don't be angered by my words. Just because you have a
free city, don't make an arrogant answer when yours is the weaker case. For hope
480 is not a thing you can trust; it has embroiled many a state, by arousing excessive
ambition. For when the question of war is brought to the popular vote, no man
thinks yet of his own death, but averts this threat and hopes it will fall upon
another's head. But if death were in full view during the vote, Greece would
485 never have been ruining herself with her lust for war. And yet we all know the
better of the two arguments, what is good (<u>chrēstos</u>) and what is evil, and how
much better is peace for men than war. For Peace, the Muses' dearest friend
490 but the enemy of Vengeance, delights to be blessed with fine children and rejoices
in prosperity. But we disregard all this and perversely embark on wars, and we
men consign to slavery the man who comes off worse, and one city imposes that
same fate on another.

Praise for the Middle Classes

> Despite his enthusiasm for democracy, Theseus has previously revealed
> in a speech to Adrastus that he is no extremist.

Euripides, Suppliants 229-245

Theseus:- But by leading out all the Argives to war, despite the divine warnings
230 uttered by the prophets, you dishonoured and wilfully flouted the gods, and so
ruined the city. You were led astray by those young men who delight in gaining
honour for themselves, and, without regard to justice, promote wars and corrupt
their fellow-citizens. One aspires to the command of armies, another to win power and
235 the licence (<u>hubris</u>) that goes with it, yet another aims for personal profit,
ignoring the harm that the <u>plēthos</u> may thus suffer. For citizens may be divided
into three groups: the wealthy, useless and always longing for more; and the
240 have-nots, living on subsistence level, dangerous men, overfull of envy, who, when
beguiled by the tongues of common (<u>ponēroi</u>) prostatai, shoot out bitter barbs
245 against the rich; but of the three, it is the middle rank that saves cities, by preserving
the order which the city ordains.

Democracy - A Part of Aristotle's Analysis

> ARISTOTLE (384-322) was in Athens from c.367 until Plato's death in 346,
> as a student and later as a teacher of a wide range of subjects at Plato's
> academy. Later, in his native Macedonia, he became, for a short time,
> tutor to the future Alexander the Great, before returning to Athens (336-323)
> to set up his own school, the Lyceum. The Politics - 'Man in Society' -
> contains a study of democratic institutions in which Aristotle virtually repro-
> duces the features of the Athenian democracy of his own day. But we may
> take the following passage as a fair description of Periclean democracy,
> apart from the payment of the Assembly which was not introduced until c.392.

Aristotle, Politics 1317b 17 - 1318a 10

From the above (i.e. the belief that liberty and equality are the foundations of democracy), especially in the matter of the control of power, are derived the following features of democracy.   All offices (archai) are open to anyone by election.   The majority rules over the individual, but each individual has his
20   chance of power.   All elections to office are by lot, or at any rate those which do not call for some particular experience or training.   There is no property-qualification, or only a minimal one.   The same man is not to hold an office twice, or only rarely, with a few exceptions, notably military.   Tenure of all
25   offices, or as many as possible, is for a short term.   Jury-service on all, or most, matters is open to all, and always in the case of the most important and authoritative decisions, such as euthūnai and questions of citizenship (politeia) and contracts between individuals.   The Assembly is sovereign in everything.   No office has sovereign power in any matter, or only in minor
30   ones, or else the Council has sovereign power over the most important issues: of all offices, membership of the Council is the most democratic, insofar as the citizens do not all receive pay: for pay all round takes the power even from this body: for if well paid for its services, the dēmos takes over the handling of all disputed business, as explained above .   Payment for service is the rule in the
35   Assembly, the jury-courts and offices, or at least in the offices, jury-courts, Principal Assemblies (kuriai ekklēsiai). or any offices where communal meals have to be taken.   Just as high birth, wealth and education (paideia) are the
40   marks of oligarchy, so their opposites are regarded as democratic, namely low birth (ageneia), poverty and vulgarity (banausia).   There are no offices held in
1318a   perpetuity, and if any such office survives from an earlier regime, it is usually shorn of its power and its holders are chosen by lot from selected candidates.

These then are the common features in democracies.   And from the idea of
5   justice that is generally accepted as democratic, namely that based on numerical equality, arises what seems to be the most genuine democracy and dēmos: equality such that rich and poor exercise equal power in government, no individuals having sovereign power, but all sharing it together on an equal
10   numerical basis.   In this way they think that they produce equality and liberty in the constitution.

> Aristotle then goes on to distinguish four kinds of democracy, making
> his division according to the occupation of the citizens.   His description
> of agricultural and pastoral democracies is universally true of such
> communities.

Aristotle, Politics 1318b 6 - 1319a 38

Of the four types of democracy. the best is the one which comes first in order, as has been stated above.   It is also the oldest.   This classification is by types of dēmos.   An agricultural community is the best (beltistos) dēmos, so that
10   democracy is possible wherever the plēthos live from farming or stockbreeding. Since there is no superfluous wealth. they are too busy for frequent meetings of the Assembly. but because they have the necessities of life, they mind their own
15   affairs and do not covet their neighbours' possessions.   Working on the land is more pleasant to them than the cares of government and political life, so long as there is no great gain to be made out of holding office.   For most men are more interested in profit than in prestige.   A sign of this is that they used to put up with tyrannies in former times, and still bear with oligarchies now, as long as their means of livelihood is not denied them or their property
20   taken away.   Some of them quickly grow wealthy, and the others are at least not in actual want.   Indeed, to have the power to vote at elections or to take part in euthūnai makes up for the lack, if any of them nurse political ambitions.   For in some democracies, even when they have no part in the choice of officials, but an electoral board is selected from all the citizens by turns, as at Mantinea,
25   nonetheless if they are entitled to make policy, the majority are content enough; and we must think of this as a form of democracy, as it was at Mantinea.

And so it is both customary and convenient in this type of democracy of which we have been talking, that all should be electors and jurors and take part in
30   the euthūnai, but that those who occupy the most important offices should be

Page 2

elected and possess a property-qualification, in proportion to the importance of their office; or else ability, and not property, should be used as the qualification for office. In this way the governing of the country is sure to be good; for the offices will always be in the hands of the best men, in
35 accordance with the wishes of the dēmos, who will not envy the moderate aristocrats (epieikeis). Meanwhile this form of government will satisfy those moderates (epieikeis) and men of note (gnōrimoi), for they will not be ruled by their inferiors, while their rule will be just, since they can be subjected to euthūnai by the others. This interdependence, and the fact that no one may act
40 simply to please himself, is an advantage. For the freedom (exousia) to do just as one
1319 a pleases means that there is no safeguard against the meaner element in human nature. This kind of democracy, then, ensures what is an invaluable feature of any constitution: government by moderate (epieikeis), uncorrupt aristocrats, without detriment to the plēthos.
5 It is clear, then, that this is the best of the democracies, for this reason, that it depends on the best dēmos. As for how to make your dēmos farmers, some of the laws handed down from former times are very useful, such as the prohibition of land-acquisition beyond a certain amount, or restriction within certain areas at a
10 given distance from the town where the central government is situated. In many cities it was laid down that the original allotments of land were inalienable; there is also the so-called law of Oxylus, which has much the same effect. It prohibits the raising of a mortgage beyond a certain sum on land belonging to an individual.
15 Nowadays we ought to reform things by also applying the law of the Aphytaeans, which is most useful for what I was describing. For although they are numerous and possess only a little land, the Aphytaeans are all farmers. They are assessed not on whole properties, but on fractions so small that even the poor exceed the minimum.
20 Next to an agricultural plēthos, the best dēmos is one which earns its living from herding and rearing livestock. There are many points of resemblance to the farmers; indeed in war they are better, since they are well-trained in their disposition and are physically fit and can live in the open. All other types of
25 plēthos, I suppose, of which the other sorts of democracies are made up, are greatly inferior to these. Their way of life is mean and their work lacks any excellence (aretē). They are a plēthos of layabouts, vulgar manual workers (banausoi), and labourers (thētes), and because men of this class are constantly hanging about in the city and around the Agora, they find it far too easy to
30 come to the Assembly. The farmers, on the other hand, are scattered throughout the countryside, and so they neither appear at meetings nor find them necessary to the same extent. And when the layout of the country is such that the farmland is
35 far away from the city, it is easy to construct a sound (chrēstos) democracy and politeia. For the plēthos must make their homes out in the country, so that even if there is an urban (agoraios) rabble (ochlos), it ought not to dominate the democratic meetings of the Assembly in the absence of the rural plēthos.

Aristotle thought that democracy was a degenerate form of what he calls politeia, i.e. a cross between democracy and oligarchy. Such a mixture was Aristotle's ideal. Cf. Thucydides' opinion at 8.97.2. (P. 547).

Aristotle. Politics 1289 a 26-30

In our original enquiry into constitutions, we distinguished three straightforward constitutions, kingship, meritocracy (aristocratia), and politeia, and three perversions of these, tyranny, of kingship, oligarchy, of meritocracy
30 (aristocratia), and democracy, of politeia.

In the following passage Aristotle makes another fourfold division of democracy, this time according to the degree of licence given to the dēmos.

-5-

Aristotle. Politics 1291 b 30 - 1292 a 38

30 The primary variety of democracy is based on the principle of equality. The
law of such a democracy insists that neither rich nor poor shall have undue
influence, nor shall either group predominate, but both shall be equal.   For
35 if, as some insist, freedom is especially to be found in democracies, and
likewise equality, this is most likely to be true when all take the same share
in the politeia.   Since the dēmos is the more numerous and the judgement
of the majority is sovereign, this must be democracy.   There are four forms
40 of democracy: the first when holding of offices is dependent on a property-
qualification, which should be small.   Anyone who possesses this must be
permitted a share in political life, and anyone who loses it must be denied
1292 a his share.   The second form of democracy is when all citizens have a share,
2 unless they fail to pass a scrutiny as to birth (anhypeuthūnoi), but law is
supreme.   The third version has everyone taking a share in office, provided
only that he is a citizen, and again the law is supreme.   The fourth kind is
5 exactly the same as this, except that the plēthos is sovereign and not the law.
This happens when decrees (psēphismata) can overrule the laws - a situation
brought about by demagogues (dēmagōgoi).   When states are democratically
governed in accordance with the rule of law, the demagogue does not exist;
the 'best' (beltistoi) citizens are in the front seat.   Where the law is not supreme,
10 then there are demagogues.   The demos becomes monarchical, a single ruler
composed of many people.   For it is collectively, not individually, that the
multitude (hoi polloi) is sovereign.   When Homer (Iliad 2. 203ff.) said that
multiple rule was a bad thing, I am not sure whether he meant this or rule by
15 more than one ruler, each out for himself.   The quasi-monarchical dēmos,
such as this, seeks to rule as a monarch, because it is not itself subject to
the rule of law, and it becomes dictatorial (despotikos) and favours those that
flatter it.   Hence such a dēmos is the counterpart of tyranny among monarchies.
Even its character is the same.   Both act as dictators over the better class
20 of citizen (beltiones), and the decrees (psēphismata) of one are like the
ordinances of the other.   The flatterer of the tyrant is the counterpart to the
demagogue, since each exercises his influence in the same way, the flatterer
wheedling the tyrant, the demagogue cajoling this type of dēmos.   By
25 bringing every question before the dēmos, these men cause its decrees
(psēphismata) to become supreme, instead of the laws.   They increase their
own power, because, while the dēmos rules over all, they rule over the dēmos'
opinions; for the plēthos follows their lead.   And whenever anyone complains
about elected officials and says that the dēmos is the best judge, the demagogue
30 gladly accepts the challenge, so that all the offices are undermined.   Indeed
a man who said that such democracy was not a form of politeia at all, would
seem to be quite right.   For where the laws do not rule, there is no politeia.
There must be a rule of law over everything, and officials with control over
35 matters of detail.   Then you have politeia.   So if democracy is one of the
types of politeia, then clearly this state of affairs, in which everything is subject to decrees (psēphismata), is not even a true democracy: for a decree
(psēphisma) has no universal validity.   This then is the way to distinguish
the forms of democracy.

3.   THE ATHENIAN CONSTITUTION

The Constitution of Cleisthenes

Herodotus described Cleisthenes as "the man who set up the tribes
and democracy in Athens" (6. 131).   Here is his account of how
these changes were carried out in 508/7.

Herodotus 5. 66-67 ; 69

5. 66 Athens had been great before, and now that she was freed from her tyrants, she
grew greater still.   Two men held the chief power (dunasteuein) in the city,
Cleisthenes an Alcmaeonid, who is reputed to have seduced the Pythian
priestess, and Isagoras, son of Teisandrus, a man of a notable (dokimos)

family, but I cannot tell the history of it; but members of his fami'y sacrifice
to Carian Zeus. These men with their factions (staseis) were rivals for power, and when
Cleisthenes began to come off worse, he took the dēmos into partnership. He
then changed the number of Athenian tribes from four to ten, and abolished the
old names,– they had been called after Geleon, Aigicores, Argades and Hagles,
the sons of Ion,– and invented names taken from other heroes, all native
Athenian except Ajax, whom he added, although he was a foreigner, because

67 he was a neighbour and ally. In doing this, I think this Cleisthenes was imitating
his own mother's father, Cleisthenes the tyrant of Sicyon.

> Herodotus then describes how Cleisthenes of Sicyon changed the names
> of the tribes there, so that they would not be the same as those at Argos,
> their arch–enemy, and renamed them 'Pig-men, Donkey-men and Swine-
> men'.

69 .... The Athenian Cleisthenes did not want the Athenians and Ionians to have
the same tribes. So as soon as he had won the support of the Athenian dēmos,
which until then had been debarred from all rights, he renamed the tribes and
increased their number making ten phylarchoi (each of whom commanded a
tribe's cavalry - division) instead of the original four, and allotting ten demes
(dēmoi) to each tribe. And when he had won the support of the dēmos, he was
far stronger than the rival stasis.

> The writer of the 'CONSTITUTION OF ATHENS' (Athēnaiōn Politeia),
> was more likely a research student under his tutorship than Aristotle
> himself. Chapters 1–41 on earlier history seem to be based on earlier
> works about Athens, but without careful assessment of the value of the
> various sources. The account of the events of 411 was inf'uenced by
> oligarchic propaganda (or perhaps by Antiphon's speech, p. 41). The
> 'Constitution of Athens' was written between 328 and 325, and only the
> later chapters dealing with the constitution in the fourth century are
> sufficiently accurate to be accepted without suspicion; these earlier
> chapters must be read with considerable caution.

Aristotle, Constitution of Athens 21. 1-4

1 Then when Cleisthenes had become prostatēs of the plēthos, three years after
2 the overthrow of the tyrants, in the year of the archonship of Isagoras (508/7),
he first divided the whole population into ten tribes instead of four, with the
aim of mixing them up so that a greater number might share in the politeia.
This was the origin of the saying:- 'Don't look at the tribes', which was
3 directed at those who want to enquire into men's family background. Secondly,
he set up a Council of Five Hundred instead of the existing Council of Four
Hundred, taking fifty from each tribe, instead of one hundred (from each of
the four previous tribes). He did not arrange them into twelve tribes because
he wanted to avoid a division according to the already existing trittyes (thirds).
For the four tribes contained twelve trittyes, and so this would not have led to a
4 new mixture of the plēthos. He also divided the country by demes (dēmoi) into
thirty parts, ten from the city region (peri to astu), ten along the coast (paralia)
and ten inland (mesogeios). These parts he called trittyes, and assigned three
of them by lot to each tribe, so that each tribe would have one portion from each
region. He made the inhabitants in each of the demes fellow-demesmen, so that
they would not address one another by their fathers' names, thus exposing new
citizens, but would call people by the names of their demes. That indeed is why
the Athenians speak of one another by the names of their demes.

Pay

Aristotle, Constitution of Athens 24.3

3 From the tribute (phoroi) and the dues (telē) and the allies, it came about that
more than 20,000 men were maintained. There were 6,000 jurymen, 1600 archers,
and in addition 1200 cavalrymen, the Council of Five Hundred, 500 dockyard-guards
as well as 50 guards on the Acropolis, about 700 minor officials at home and about
(?) 700 abroad. On top of these, when they went to war later, there were 2,500

hoplites, 20 guard-ships, and 2,000 men, chosen by lot, on the other ships which brought the tribute (phoroi). And besides, there were the Town Hall (prytaneion), the orphans, and the prison-warders. All these were maintained out of public funds.

Citizenship Law

The benefits of Periclean democracy were jealously guarded. Cf. Aristotle, Politics, 1292a 2, p.6; Aristophanes, Frogs 686ff., p.55; and Wasps 718, p.26.

Aristotle, Constitution of Athens 26.4

4 Two years later, in the archonship of Antidotus (451/0), because of the large number (plēthos) of citizens, they decided, on the proposal of Pericles, that no one should have the citizenship unless both his parents had been citizens.

Pay for Jurymen (dicasts)

Aristotle, Constitution of Athens 27, 4-5

4 Pericles ... instituted payment for jurymen. Some people blame him for this and say that they deteriorated, because it was always the ordinary men (hoi tychontes) rather than the moderate aristocrats (epieikeis) who took care to
5 cast lots for jury-service. After this, bribery also began; the first instance was that of Anytus after his command as General (stratēgos) at Pylos (in 409); he bribed the court and was acquitted, when he was prosecuted for losing Pylos.

Ostracism

PLUTARCH (c.46-120 A.D.) was not so much a historian as a biographer. He is often careless in his chronology, in judging his authorities, and in letting his own political opinions influence his interpretation of characters and events. Nevertheless, he appears in the following passage to give a better (though moralizing) account of the purpose of ostracism than Aristotle, Constitution of Athens 22, and a fuller (and apparently accurate) version of Hyperbolus' ostracism than Thucydides 8.73 (P. 529).

Plutarch, Aristides 7, 3-8

3 Ostracism was not a punishment for any wickedness (mochthēria). While for political reasons it was called 'a lowering and curtailing of arrogance and excessive power', it was in fact a humane appeasement of envy, resulting in no irreparable harm, but in removing for ten years the hostility of any person bent on causing
4 trouble. But when some people began to exercise it against low-born (agenneis) and common (ponēroi) men, ostracism was brought to an end, the last case being
5 that of Hyperbolus. The cause of Hyperbolus' ostracism is said to have been as follows:- Alcibiades and Nicias, who were the most powerful men (dunamenoi) in the state, were at odds. So when the dēmos was about to vote the ostracism, and clearly would decree it against one of them, they consulted together and by uniting their respective parties (staseis) contrived the ostracism of Hyperbolus.
6 As a result of this, the dēmos were indignant that the business had been conducted with such hubris and had been brought into disrepute, and they put an end to
7 ostracism altogether and abolished it. The procedure, to put it briefly, was this:- Each man took an 'ostrakon' (a piece of broken pottery) and wrote on it the name of the citizen he wished to remove; then he took it to a part of the Agora that was
8 surrounded with railings. The archons first totalled up the number of all the ostraka put together; if those who had taken part numbered less than six thousand, the ostracism was void. They then put each name by itself and declared the man whose name had been written most times as banished for ten years, though not deprived of his possessions.

The Council (boulē) and the Assembly (ekklēsia)

N.B. In the fifth century, the prytaneis and their own epistatēs (1) presided at the Assembly. The prohedroi and their own epistatēs (2), mentioned in 44.2-3, were not established until c.378.

Aristotle, Constitution of Athens 43.2 - 45.4

2   The Council of Five Hundred is chosen by lot, fifty members from each tribe.
     Each tribe takes it in turn to provide the prytaneis, in an order settled by lot,
     each of the first four tribes for thirty-six days, and each of the last six for
3   thirty-five days; for they divide up their year into lunar months. Those
     who serve as prytaneis firstly dine together in the Tholos, receiving money from
     the state, and secondly call meetings of the Council and Assemblies of the dēmos;
     the Council meets on every day except holidays, and the dēmos assembles four
     times during each prytany. The prytaneis give written notice in advance of the
     business to be transacted by the Council, both what is to be done on each day
4   and where they are to meet. They also give written notice in advance of meetings
     of the Assembly; one meeting, the Principal Assembly (kuria ekklēsia), is the one
     at which they are required to vote for the confirmation of officials if they appear
     to be governing well, and to deal with the food supply and the defence of the
     country; anyone who wishes to bring an impeachment (eisangelia) must do so on
     this day; inventories of estates being confiscated must also be read and legal
     claims for the right of succession to inheritances and of marriage to an heiress,
     so that everyone may have the opportunity to learn of any vacancy in an estate.
5   During the sixth prytany, in addition to the specified business, they take a vote
     on whether they should hold an ostracism or not; and also vote on preliminary
     information laid against anyone, Athenian citizen or metic, accused of being a
     sycophant, up to three cases in each class; in addition, they consider any cases
6   where promises made to the dēmos have not been kept. The second Assembly (in
     each prytany) is devoted to petitions; at this meeting anyone who wishes may lay
     down a suppliant branch, and then address the dēmos on any subject he wishes,
     whether private or public. The other two Assemblies (in each prytany) deal with
     any other business; at these the laws lay down that three cases of sacred matters
     are to be dealt with, three cases concerning heralds and embassies, and three
     cases concerning secular matters. Sometimes they transact business without a
     preliminary vote (procheirotonia). Heralds and ambassadors approach the
     prytaneis first, and those who carry dispatches also deliver them to these men.
44.1 One of the prytaneis is chosen by lot to be chairman (epistatēs(1)); he holds
     this position for a night and a day, and he may not hold it longer nor hold the
     same position twice. He keeps the keys of the temples in which public funds
     and documents are kept, and he keeps the state seal; he and a third of the
     number of the prytaneis, whichever third he nominates, are required to stay in
2   the Tholos. When the prytaneis convoke the Council or the Assembly of the dēmos,
     the chairman (epistatēs(1)) appoints by lot nine presiding officers (prohedroi), one
     from each tribe except the one that is holding the prytany at that time, and from
     these in turn he appoints a single chairman (epistatēs(2)), and hands over to
3   these prohedroi a list of agenda. When they receive the agenda, the prohedroi
     superintend procedure, bring forward the business which is to be dealt with,
     check the voting and direct all other business; they are also authorised to
     dismiss the Assembly. A man cannot become chairman (epistatēs(2)) more
4   than once a year, but he may be prohedros once in each prytany. The prytaneis
     also conduct in the Assembly the elections of Generals (stratēgoi), cavalry
     commanders (hipparchoi), and other military officers, according to the decision
     of the dēmos. These elections take place in the first prytany after the sixth one,
     during which favourable weather-signs occur. There must also be a preliminary
     resolution of the Council (probouleuma) with regard to these matters.
45.1 Formerly (i.e. before 403), the Council had authority to impose fines and sentences
     of imprisonment and death....
2   Most trials of officials, particularly of those who handle money, are judged by the
     Council; their verdict, however, is not sovereign, but is subject to appeal to
     the jury-court. Private individuals also have the right to bring an impeachment
     (eisangelia) against any official for illegal conduct; and in these cases also, the
3   officials can appeal to the jury-court if the Council finds them guilty. The Council
     also checks the qualifications (dokimasia) of the Councillors and the nine archons
     for the following year. Formerly it had the power to disqualify them, but now
4   they may appeal to the jury-court. Thus in these matters the Council does not
     have supreme power, but it frames preliminary resolutions (probouleumata) for
     the dēmos, and the dēmos cannot vote on any measure that has not been prepared

by the Council in this way and of which the prytaneis have not given advance
notice in writing; for anyone who brings in a bill in violation of these rules
is liable to an action for illegal procedure (graphē paranomōn).

The Generals (stratēgoi)

N.B. In the fifth century, the allotment of separate provinces to each
General did not occur

Aristotle, Constitution of Athens 61. 1-2

1   They (the dēmos) also elect by show of hands all military officers, including
the ten Generals (stratēgoi); in former times one from each tribe, but now
(i.e. in the fourth century) from the whole citizen body; they also assign their
various duties by a show of hands. One becomes commander of the hoplites
and leads them when they go out on a foreign expedition. Another becomes
chief of the home-guard, and if there is a war within the borders of the country,
he takes charge of the war-effort. Two are responsible for the Piraeus, one
of them for Munichia, the other for Actē, and they take care of the defence of
the Piraeus . One is responsible for the symmories (groups of rich citizens
formed in 377 to share the burden of liturgies which were too expensive for
an individual to bear), and appoints the trierarchs and arranges exchanges of
property for them, and brings before the jury-court any disputes arising from
these obligations. The rest of the Generals are assigned to whatever matters
2   may need to be dealt with at the time. In each prytany there is a vote on whether
each General's conduct in office appears to be satisfactory. and if they vote
against any of them, he is then tried in the jury-court If he is found guilty, they
fix his punishment or fine; but if he is acquitted, he returns to office. When on
campaign, the Generals have authority to arrest a man for indiscipline, to cashier
him, and to impose a fine. But they do not usually impose fines.

4.   ATHENS IDEALIZED

The Funeral Speech of Pericles in honour of the Athenians who died in
battle in 431 is largely a panegyric on Athenian democracy at its zenith.

See Thucydides 2. 36-46 (P. 116-123).

The Imports of Athens

.is is a fragment from the comedian HERMIPPUS, written between 430
and 424.   The style is mock-heroic.

Hermippus, Phormophoroi. Fragment

Tell me now, you Muses who have dwelt in the halls of Olympus, ever since
Dionysus has owned a ship on the wine-dark sea, what goods he has brought for
men here in his black ship. From Cyrene he has brought silphium and ox-hide.
5   and from the Hellespont fresh fish and all sorts of fish which are then dried;
while from Italy come grains of wheat and sides of beef, not to mention from
Sitalces scurvy for the Spartans, and from Perdiccas lies by the armada.
10   Syracuse provides pigs and cheese. and I wish Poseidon would destroy the
Corcyraeans in their hollow ships, because they disagree with us! That's all
we get from them. but from Egypt come hanging sails and papyrus. and from
Syria frankincense. Beautiful Crete provides cypress-wood for (the shrines of) the
15   Gods. while Libya provides quantities of ivory for sale. Rhodes obliges with
raisins and figs that bring on sweet dreams. Besides. from Euboea come pears
and big juicy apples. and from Phrygia slaves. and from Arcadia allies. Pagasae
20   gives slaves and runaways. The Paphlagonians send chestnuts and glittering
almonds. which will be the delight of a feast. Phoenicia grows dates for us and
makes a fine wheat flour. and Carthage provides carpets and embroidered cushions.

Athens the Brilliant

Euripides includes this beautiful song in praise of his native city, Athens, at
a tense moment in the play. where Medea has outlined her plan to kill her own
children. and then to accept an earlier offer of asylum in Athens. The play
was produced in 431.

Euripides, Medea 824-845

Chorus of Corinthian Women:- From of old the children of Erechtheus (i.e. the
825   Athenians) have been fortunate, sons of the blessed gods. They trace their
origin to a sacred and unconquered land, where they feed on her far-famed
830   wisdom (sophia) ; and for ever pass gracefully through the most brilliant air,
where once, men say, the nine pure Muses of Pieria gave birth to golden Harmony.
835   And beside the fair-flowing stream of Cephisus, the Cyprian goddess (Aphroditē)
is said to have drawn water and breathed upon the land sweet and gentle breezes;
840   on her hair all this time lay a sweet-scented garland of roses as she was escorted
by the Loves, who sit at the side of Wisdom (sophia) and help men to achieve
845   every kind of excellence (aretē).

Plutarch on Periclean Athens

Plutarch is here in agreement with Thucydides' judgement of Pericles
as a moderate leader (Thucydides 2.65.5 (P.134)), and counters the
hostile views of his fourth-century authorities. Plato (e.g. Gorgias
515 E, p. 14), Ephorus, Theopompus and the political pamphleteers,
who describe him as a demagogue pandering to the wishes of the people.

Plutarch, Pericles 11-12

11.1   The aristocrats (aristokratikoi), seeing that Pericles had already become the
greatest of the citizens, but nevertheless wanting someone to be set up against
him in the city and to blunt his power, so that it was not altogether a monarchy,
set up Thucydides from Alōpekē, a moderate (sōphrōn) man and a kinsman of
Cimon, to oppose him; he was less skilled in war than Cimon, yet a more
skilful speaker and politician, and by staying in Athens and engaging with
Pericles on the platform. he quickly brought the politeia to a state of balance.

2   For he did not allow the true gentlemen (kaloi k'agathoi) to be scattered and
mixed among the dēmos as before, with their reputation eclipsed by the plethos;
but taking them apart and uniting them in the same area (of the Pnyx), he made
their combined power influential like the counterpoise on a balance. For there was from
the beginning a sort of hidden split. as in a piece of iron, marking a difference
between the policies of the dēmos and those of the aristocrats, and the contention
and rivalry between them cut a deep gash in the city and caused one side to be

3   called democrats and the other oligarchs. And so it was just at that time that
Pericles let loose the reins to the dēmos and governed the state according to
its pleasure; he was always contriving some festive spectacle or banquet or
procession in the town and tutoring the city with pleasures that were not
uncultured (amousoi) ; and besides this he sent out sixty triremes each year,
in which sailed many of the citizens, serving for pay for eight months and at

4   the same time practising and learning the art of seamanship. In addition, he sent a
thousand men as settlers (cleruchs) to the Chersonese, five hundred to Naxos,
half this number to Andros, a thousand to Thrace to dwell among the Bisaltae.
and others to Italy when Sybaris. which they renamed Thurii, was colonised.
By doing this, he was relieving the city of a lazy, and as a result of their idleness,
a meddlesome (polypragmōn) rabble (ochlos), and was settling the difficult
circumstances of the dēmos, as well as establishing fear and a garrison among
the allies so that they would not attempt any political changes (neōterizein).

12.1   But what brought most pleasure and adornment to Athens, and the greatest
admiration from all other men, a thing which is now Greece's only witness
that Athens does not lie about her much-vaunted power and her former wealth,
was his construction of temples and public buildings; and yet this most of
all the policies of Pericles was criticised and slanged in the Assemblies by
his enemies, who insisted; "The dēmos is losing its fine reputation and is
being attacked for having removed the common Treasury of the Greeks from
Delos into its own custody. Pericles has not left himself even his most
specious of excuses against his accusers, namely that he removed the common
Treasury from Delos for fear of the Persians and is now safeguarding it. And
it appears that Greece is suffering a dire insult (hubris) and is the victim of
open tyranny, when she sees the special levies (eisphorai) she has been obliged
to contribute towards the war being lavished by us in gilding our city and
ornamenting it, like some hussey of a woman, being decked out with precious
stones and statues and temples that cost a thousand talents".

2   So Pericles began to instruct the dēmos and said they did not owe their allies an account of the money as long as they fought on their behalf and kept the barbarians at a distance; for their allies contributed no horses, no ships, no <u>hoplites</u>, but only money, which belonged not to the givers, but to those who received it, as long as they carried out the object for which they received it. "Since the city is sufficiently provided with all that is necessary for the war, it is right to turn its surplus to those objects which, when they are completed, will bring eternal glory, and which, while they are being constructed, will be a ready source of prosperity, since every kind of workmanship will be on view and those manifold necessities which, by stimulating every art <u>(technē)</u> and employing every hand, will put almost the whole city in pay, while at the

3   same time it is being adorned and maintained from its own resources". For to those of military age and strength the armies provided ample resources from the common funds, and, since he wanted the mechanics <u>(banausoi)</u> and the unruly rabble (ochlos) to have their share of the profits, and yet not to receive it when idle or unoccupied, he therefore brought to the dēmos vast building projects and intricate work plans which kept them fully occupied, so that those staying at home would have as good a reason for receiving assistance from the public funds and taking their share, as those at sea or on garrison-duty or in the army.

4   For the different materials such as stone, bronze, ivory, gold, ebony, and cypress-wood, and for the arts (technai) that fashion and work them, there were carpenters, moulders, braziers, masons, dyers, workers in gold and ivory, painters, embroiderers and turners. To carry and convey these materials, there were merchants, sailors and helmsmen, by sea, and on land cartwrights, cattlemen, drivers, ropemakers, flax-workers, boot-makers, road-builders and miners. And just as a general has his own army, so every trade (technē) had its gang of unskilled labourers <u>(thētikos ochlos)</u> organised, the instrument and body of manual service. Thus, in brief, these requirements brought about the spreading and distribution of prosperity amongst men of every age and character.

The Humble Private Houses of the Fifth Century

The Athenian orator DEMOSTHENES, born in 384, makes occasional incidental references in his speeches to conditions in the previous century. Another similar comment on fifth century houses occurs in Demosthenes, Olynthiacs 3. 25-26.

Demosthenes, Against Aristocrates 689 (delivered in 352)

In those days the state was wealthy and splendid, but in private life no man stood out above the multitude (hoi polloi). Here is the proof: if any of you knows the sort of house that Themistocles or Miltiades or any of the distinguished men of those times lived in, he sees that it is no grander than the houses of the multitude (hoi polloi); while the public works and buildings were on such a scale and of such a quality that no opportunity of surpassing them is left to any succeeding generation. There is the Propylaea here, the docks, porticoes, the Piraeus, and all the other works with which you see the city adorned.

ISOCRATES (436-338), the fourth century orator, political thinker and essayist, tells us in the course of this political pamphlet, written in 355, that considerable sums of money were spent on country-houses in the fifth century. Cf. Thucydides 2.65.2 (P. 134).

Isocrates, Areopagiticus 52

.... (our forefathers) lived in such a state of security that the houses and buildings in the countryside were finer and more costly than those inside the city-walls, and many of the citizens did not come into Athens even for the festivals....

5.   THE IMPACT OF MIGRATION AND THE PLAGUE (431–430)

See Thucydides 2.14 (P. 106) ; 16 (P.107); 17.1 & 3 (P. 107-8); 52-53 (P. 126-7).

6.   PERICLES AT BAY: ESTIMATES OF HIM AND HIS SUCCESSORS

Revulsion against Pericles and his policy came in the summer of 430. Pericles replied with an imperialist supplement to the Funeral Speech.

See Thucydides 2. 59-65 (P. 129-135).

Two Views of Pericles

Besides Aristophanes, the leading Greek comic poets of the fifth century were CRATINUS (c. 484 - c.420) and EUPOLIS (c.455 - c.410).   In the following fragment, Cratinus mockingly alludes to Pericles' sensitivity about the elongated shape of his head, as well as to his narrow escape from ostracism in 444.   By contrast, Eupolis looks back admiringly upon Pericles the public speaker.

Cratinus, Fragment, OBGV No. 298

Here comes Pericles, our squill-headed Zeus, with a hat like the Albert Hall (Odeion) on his head, now that all the tiles on the houses have been used for the ostracism.

Eupolis, Fragment, OBGV No. 440

Pericles surpassed all other men as an orator: whenever he rose to speak, it was as if, like a crack runner, he had given the other runners a ten-foot start and then overtook them.   What is more, apart from his speed, there was persuasion that sat upon his lips: with it he cast spells and was the only one of the speakers (rhētores) to leave behind him his sting, implanted in the audience.

'Aristotle' on the Leaders of the People (Prostatai tou dēmou)

Note the oligarchic flavour of this passage (see p. 7).

Aristotle, Constitution of Athens 28.1; 3-5

28.1   While Pericles was prostatēs tou dēmou, the affairs of state went better, but after his death they became much worse.   For the dēmos now for the first time chose a prostatēs who was not of good reputation among the moderate aristocrats (epieikeis);   whereas in former times these epieikeis had always continued to lead the dēmos (demagōgein). . . . .

3   When Pericles died, Nicias, who, later died in Sicily, became the prostatēs of the men of distinction (epiphaneis), and Cleon, son of Cleainetus, became prostatēs tou dēmou; this man, more than any other, seems to have corrupted the dēmos by his violent methods, and was the first to shout on the platform, to use abusive language, and to speak with his cloak girt up about him, while all other men spoke in decent fashion.   Then after these men, Thēramenes, son of Hagnon, was leader of one party, while Cleophon, the lyremaker, was the leader of the dēmos; it was he who first introduced the diōbelia. He had this distributed for some time, but afterwards Callicrates from Paeania displaced him, being the first to promise to add another obol to the other two. Later, however, both these men were condemned to death.   For even if the plēthos has been deceived, it usually afterwards hates those who have led it

4   to do anything improper.   After Cleophon, the leadership of the dēmos (dēmagōgia) was now held in succession by those men who were most willing to play the part boldly and to court the favour of the multitude (hoi polloi),

5   always viewing things in the short term. After the men of the early period, the
best men (beltistoi) to govern Athens seem to have been Nicias, Thucydides and
Theramenes. As for Nicias and Thucydides, there is almost universal
agreement that they were not only true gentlemen (kaloi k'agathoi), but also
statesmen and patriotic servants of the whole city: about Theramenes opinion
is divided, because of the turbulent politics of the time. But if one is to avoid
a superficial judgement of him, he seems not to have tried to overthrow all
constitutions, as his detractors declare, but to have been trying to develop
them all, so long as they remained within the legal framework; for he was
able to serve the state under all constitutions, which is the duty of a good
citizen, but would rather incur hostility than submit to them when they acted
illegally.

Plato's Criticism of Pericles' Leadership

PLATO was born c.428 and died c.348. Although he did not set
out to be a historian, and is sometimes as unfair in his criticisms
of individuals as he is unreliable in matters of chronology, there
is no reason to doubt the accuracy of his general account of the
sophists' teaching, (especially in the Protagoras), or to minimise
the value of his satire on Athenian democracy (Republic 557 A, ff., p.57).
It is notoriously hard to distinguish between the views of Socrates
and the views of Plato himself. Broadly speaking, the earlier the
dialogue the more likely it is to contain the views of Socrates. The
approximate dates of the dialogues quoted in this book, and their
respective dramatic backgrounds are:-

Dialogue	Written	Background
Protagoras	395 ?	c.435
Apology	395 ?	399
Crito	395 ?	399
Gorgias	390 ?	424
Meno	390 ?	403
Republic	387 ?	424 ? or later.

In the following passage Plato represents Socrates as the only true
statesman in Athens. (See also Gorgias 521 D, p.32). He maintains
that Pericles failed to give any moral education to the Athenian people.

Plato, Gorgias 515 B - 516 D

515 B   Callicles:-   You always want to come out best in the argument, Socrates.
         Socrates:-   That is not at all the spirit in which I ask. I really want to know
how, exactly, you think a politician should behave in Athens. Are you really
C   suggesting that if you engage in politics you will have any other purpose than
the good condition of your fellow citizens? Have we not often before now
agreed that this should be the politician's purpose? Well, haven't we? I see
I must answer for you - we have. Very well then, this being the proper purpose
of the good man towards his own city, cast your mind back to the men you were
speaking about a short while ago and tell me whether you still think they were
D   good citizens, - Pericles, I mean, and Cimon and Miltiades and Themistocles.
         Callicles:-   I do.
         Socrates:-   Well, if they were good, obviously each one of them must have made
his fellow citizens better than before. Did they?
         Callicles:-   Yes.
         Socrates:-   Then at the time of Pericles' first speeches in the Assembly (demos)
were the Athenians worse than at the time of his last speeches?
         Callicles:-   Possibly.
         Socrates:-   There's no 'possibly' about it, my dear fellow. On our premises
they must have been, that is to say if Pericles was a good citizen.
E   Callicles:-   Well?
         Socrates:-   No matter. But now proceed to answer me this. Do men say that
the Athenians were made better (beltiones) by Pericles or exactly the opposite,
that they were corrupted? What I hear is that he made them idle and cowardly

and garrulous and money-loving, being the first man to introduce payment for state-service.

Callicles:- You get that from the men with the cauliflower ears, Socrates.

Socrates:- Well, here is something which is not hearsay any longer and which you know is true as well as I do. At first the Athenians thought well of Pericles and brought no shaming charges against him in the days when they were worse: but when, thanks to him, they had become true gentlemen (kaloi k'agathoi),

516 A then at the end of his life they brought a charge of embezzlement against him and very nearly condemned him to death, obviously because they regarded him as worthless (poneros).

Callicles:- Is that supposed to prove that Pericles was bad?

Socrates:- Similar results would certainly be a proof of the incompetence of a man looking after donkeys, say, or horses or cattle, that is to say if he took them over with no inclination to kick him or butt him or bite him and by the time he had finished with them they were savage enough to do all three.

B Or perhaps you don't agree that any guardian of any living creature is a bad guardian if he finds them gentle and leaves them savage?

Callicles:- To humour you, I'll agree.

Socrates:- Well, humour me by answering this too. Is man as much a living creature as the animals?

Callicles:- Of course.

Socrates:- And wasn't Pericles looking after men?

Callicles:- Yes.

Socrates:- In that case, in accordance with what we agreed a moment ago, shouldn't these men have become more just, thanks to him, and not more unjust,

C if, that is to say, he looked after them as a good politician should?

Callicles:- Yes.

Socrates:- Well, Homer tells us the just are gentle. Are you with him?

Callicles:- Yes.

Socrates:- Yet in the event Pericles made the Athenians clearly more savage than when he took them over, and savage towards himself at that, the last thing he can have wanted.

Callicles:- Do you want me to agree with you?

Socrates:- Yes, if you think I am speaking the truth.

Callicles:- So be it then.

Socrates:- And if he made them more savage, that means more unjust and worse?

D Callicles:- So be it.

Socrates:- So the argument has proved that Pericles was not a good politician.

Callicles:- That is your story.

7. THE DĒMOS

The Poet and the Dēmos

ARISTOPHANES (c.450-c.385) provides in his comedies a valuable source of information about the years from 425 onwards. His own standpoint is conservative, and the excesses of contemporary democracy gave him ample scope for ridicule. But beneath the comedy, his attacks on the demagogues and his pleas for peace appear to be motivated by a sincere patriotism. In this passage from the Archarnians, produced in 425, he maintains that it is the politician's duty to give the best advice, not just what the people want to hear. (Cf. Plato, Gorgias 521 D, p. 32). Since this duty was shirked by the speakers in the Assembly, it often had to be performed by the poet - and before a much larger audience.

Aristophanes, Acharnians 628-658

Chorus of Acharnians:- Since our master (i.e. Aristophanes) was first in charge of comic productions, he has never yet come to the theatre to say

630 how clever he is. But being accused by his enemies in the presence of the Athenians, rash in judgement that they are, of making a mockery of our city

and insulting the dēmos, he now has to answer in the face of Athenians, quick
to change their minds as they are.   Our poet says he deserves great reward
at your hands for having stopped you being grossly deceived by foreign words
635 and from enjoying being flattered, and from being soft-headed citizens.
Previously when ambassadors came from various cities with their deceits,
they used first of all to call you 'violet-crowned'; and whenever anyone said
this, because of those crowns, you at once sat up on the tip of your little bottoms.
And if anyone flattered you by calling Athens 'gleaming', he got everything he
640 wanted through that word 'gleaming', although applying to you the praise due
to anchovies.   By doing this and by showing the dēmoi of our allied cities how
democratically they are ruled, he has earned great reward for you.   Now
therefore, your allies will come from their cities bringing you their tribute
645 (phoros) and eager to see that excellent poet who has taken the risk of
saying in Athens what is right.   In this way the fame of his daring has
spread far, when even the Great King, in questioning the ambassadors of
Sparta, asked them first which people rules the seas, and then, regarding this
poet here, which people it is whom he warns of their many evils.   For, said he,
650 these men are far superior and will win a decisive victory in the war with this
poet to advise them.   For this reason the Spartans are offering you peace
and asking for Aegina back.   Not that they care about that island but they
655 want to take this poet for themselves.   But don't you ever let him go, since
his ridicule will be just.   And he says he will teach you much that is good, so
as to make you prosper, without flattering you or holding out promises of pay
or humbugging you; he won't play you false nor butter you up, but will teach
you all that is best.

Dēmos and his Slave

The Knights was produced in 424 when Cleon (Paphlagon) was at the height
of his power.   The theme of the play is, briefly, how a sausage-seller
out-Cleons Cleon in the favour of Dēmos, who personifies the Athenian
people.

Aristophanes, Knights 40-72

40 Demosthenes:- I'll tell you now.   Our master is Dēmos, a countryman by
temperament, a glutton for beans, quick-tempered, hard to please, getting
on in years, a little deaf, and his home is the Pnyx.   At last month's market
45 he bought a slave, a tanner called Paphlagon, an out-and-out rogue and liar.
This leathery-Paphlagon discovered the old man's tastes and began to cringe
before him and wheedle, fawn, cajole and cheat him with leather-shreds of
50 flattery, and words like these:- "Dēmos, as soon as you've got through one
verdict in the jury-court, you must have a wash, then eat up, have a good
hot drink, swallow down the sweets, and hold on to your three obols.   Would
you like me to serve a late supper for you, too?"   And then whatever food any
of us has prepared, Paphlagon steals and makes a present of it to our master.
55 The other day, when I had just struggled to knead a Spartan barley-cake at
Pylos, like the cunning rogue that he is, he slipped past me and snatched it
and served up my cake as if it was his own.   He keeps us at a distance and
60 won't let anyone else wait upon our master, but while Dēmos is dining, he
stands brandishing a leather-strap and scares away the speakers (rhētores).
He keeps singing oracles to him; he knows the old man thinks of nothing but
the Sibyl.   And when he sees him in his dotage, he performs his trick of
telling blatant lies about all of us in the household.   Then we get a beating,
65 but Paphlagon runs about among the servants laying down his demands,
creating mischief and then accepting their bribes.   "You see," he says, "how
Hylas got beaten because of me.   Make it worth my while, or today will be
70 your dying day."   So we pay up; otherwise the old man would kick the stuffing
out of us.   So now, my friend, let's decide at once what course to take and who
to turn to.

Dēmos claims not to be such a fool as he looks.   The Chorus is formed
of oligarchic Knights.

Aristophanes, Knights 1111-1130

Chorus of Knights:- O Dēmos, the sway you hold is fine indeed, seeing that
1115 all men look on you with fear as a tyrant.   Yet you are easily led by the nose;
you love to be flattered and fooled, and always gape at any speech-maker;
1120 and your mind takes a holiday!
Dēmos:- There is no mind beneath your long hair, seeing that you think I have
1125 no brains !   I act the fool like this on purpose.   I enjoy being bottle-fed all
day long, and it pleases me to fatten up a thief for a champion (prostatēs).
1130 Then when he has thoroughly gorged himself, I hoist him up and beat him up.

Plato Compares the Dēmos to a Ship's Captain

Plato, Republic 488 A-E

488 A Imagine a number of ships or, if you like, one ship: and imagine a captain in size
B and strength superior to all the crew, but a little deaf and short-sighted and
with a similarly defective knowledge of sea-faring: and picture the crew
quarrelling with each other about the control of the ship, each one claiming
to steer it himself, without ever having been taught the necessary skill (technē)
or being able to point to any trainer or period of training, all in fact alleging
that steering is not even a teachable thing and being prepared to liquidate
C anyone who says that it is: picture them always surging round the captain
himself and badgering him by entreaty or by other means to hand the tiller
to them, and, if unsuccessful, killing or throwing overboard their successful
rivals: then picture them incapacitating the noble (gennaios) captain by
mandragora or strong liquor or some other opiate and controlling the ship
and helping themselves to the cargo and drinking and feasting and sailing the
ship as you would expect such men to sail her: picture them moreover
D praising and calling 'a real sailor' or 'a real steersman' or 'a real naval man'
anyone who is good at collaborating in enabling them to control the ship by
browbeating or overpowering the captain, whereas anyone else they brand as
useless;   and as for the professional steersman, they do not even understand
his job and how he must study the yearly cycle and the seasons and the heavens
and the stars and the winds and all the other things necessary to his craft (technē),
E if he is to be genuinely capable of controlling his ship; as to how he shall steer,
let alone whether other people wish him to or not, they do not think it is possible
to acquire any such skill (technē) or training and thereby become a trained
pilot.   If this were the general state of affairs in ships, isn't it only natural
that the true pilot will be called by the sailors in such ships a stargazer and a
blatherer and a man of no use to them ?

8.   ASSEMBLY AND COUNCIL IN ACTION

A Meeting of the Assembly

Although this is a mock Assembly, the general procedure is taken from
fact.   Cf. Demosthenes, On the Crown 169-170, p. 20.

Aristophanes, Acharnians 17-173

Dicaeopolis:- Since the day I first washed myself, I have never been so
stung by soap in the eyes as today, when there's a Principal Assembly (kuria
20 ekklēsia) this morning and the Pnyx here is deserted.   They're chattering in
the Agora, edging this way and that to avoid the red rope (with which the
Archers herded loiterers into the Assembly).   Even the prytaneis aren't here
25 yet either;   they'll be late and then they'll come jostling each other for the
front row like nobody's business, flooding down in throngs.   But as for peace,
they don't care a damn for that.   O my city, my city!   And I'm always the
first to come to Assembly and take my place;   and then when I'm alone, I
30 groan and yawn and stretch, break wind and don't know what to do.   I doodle,

tear my hair and reckon my accounts, gazing at the countryside, yearning for
peace, hating town and longing for my own folk who never said 'Buy charcoal',

35 'Buy vinegar', 'Buy oil' and didn't even know the word 'buy', but produced
everything themselves and that rasping word 'buy' was left unused. So now
I have come quite prepared to shout and interrupt and slang the speakers
(rhētores) if any of them says a single word other than on the subject of

40 peace. But here are the prytaneis arriving - now that it's noon. Didn't I
tell you? This is just what I said - every man jostling for the front seat.
Crier:- Move up to the front, move inside the limits purified by ritual.

45 Amphitheus (entering late):- Has anyone spoken yet?
Crier (opening the session):- Who wishes to address the Assembly?
Amphitheus:- I do.
Crier:- Who are you?
Amphitheus:- Amphitheus.
Crier:- You're not a human being, are you?
Amphitheus:- No, I'm an Immortal; Amphitheus was the son of Demeter and
Triptolemus. Triptolemus had a son, Keleus; and he married Phaenaretē,

50 my grandmother; and she had a son, Lycīnus. I am his son and an Immortal.
It is to me alone that the gods have entrusted the task of negotiating peace with
the Spartans. But although I am an Immortal, gentlemen, I haven't any money
for my journey. For the prytaneis aren't giving any.
Crier:- Archers!

55 Amphitheus:- Triptolemus and Keleus! Will you let this happen to me?
(Amphitheus is hustled away by the Scythian Archers)
Dicaeopolis:- Prytaneis, you are acting in contempt of the Assembly by arresting
this man; he only wanted to negotiate a truce for you and to get the shields
hung up.
Crier:- Sit down! Silence!

60 Dicaeopolis:- By God, I won't! Not unless you prytaneis put the question
of peace for me.
Crier:- The ambassadors from the Great King!
(Enter the returning Athenian ambassadors, escorting the Persian envoys who
include Pseudartabas and two eunuchs; the Persians are dressed in gorgeous
oriental apparel).
Dicaeopolis:- The Great King indeed! I'm fed up with ambassadors, with all
their peacocks and humbug.
Crier:- Silence!
Dicaeopolis:- Phew! Ecbatana! What clothes!

65 Ambassador:- You sent us to the Great King with an allowance of two drachmas
a day when Euthymenes was archon (437/6. i.e. eleven years earlier).
Dicaeopolis:- O dear! So much for our drachmas!
Ambassador:- And were we fatigued wayfaring under sun-shades over the

70 Caystrian plains, reclining on soft pillows in covered carriages, utterly
fagged out!
Dicaeopolis:- Yes, and I was having it cosy amidst the filth on the battlements.
Ambassador:- And when we were entertained we were forced to drink dessert
wine neat out of crystal goblets and golden beakers.

75 Dicaeopolis:- City of Cranaus! Do you see how absurd ambassadors are?
Ambassador:- For the barbarous Persians only regard as men those who can
eat and drink the most.
Dicaeopolis:- While with us it is womanisers and perverts.

80 Ambassador:- After three years we reached the King's court; but he had gone
with his army to the bog and was spending eight months in the Golden Hills to
ease his bowels.
Dicaeopolis:- And when did he close his bowels?
Ambassador:- At the full moon: and then he came back home. Then he enter-

85 tained us, serving us with whole oxen from the pot.
Dicaeopolis:- Who ever heard of pot-baked oxen? What humbug!
Ambassador:- And he served us with a bird - as Heaven is my witness - three
times the size of Cleonymus (who was noted for his gluttony); it was called rook.

90	Dicaeopolis:-	Then that's how you rooked us of two drachmas a day.

90   Dicaeopolis:-   Then that's how you rooked us of two drachmas a day.

Ambassador:-   And now we have brought back with us Pseudartabas, the King's Eye.

Dicaeopolis:-   I wish a raven would strike out your eye - the ambassador's, I mean.

Crier:-   The King's Eye!

(Enter Pseudartabas, the King's Eye or confidential officer).

95   Dicaeopolis:-   Heaven's above! Man, have you a warlike look to the cut of your jib? Or are you just rounding the headland and scanning the dockyard? I suppose that's an oar-pad below your eye.

Ambassador:-   Now come, tell the Athenians what message the King sent you with, Pseudartabas.

100   Pseudartabas:-   Iartaman exarxan apissona satra.

Ambassador:-   Do you understand what he says?

Dicaeopolis:-   By God! I don't!

Ambassador:-   He says the King will send you gold.

(To Pseudartabas)   Speak louder and mention the gold plainly.

Pseudartabas:-   No get gold, big-arsed Ionee.

105   Dicaeopolis:-   My God! That's plain, all right.

Ambassador:-   What's he say?

Dicaeopolis:-   What's he say! He says the Ionians are big arses, if they are expecting gold from barbarians.

Ambassador:-   No, he means measures of gold.

110   Dicaeopolis:-   What measures? You're a great fraud. Clear off! I'll cross-examine him myself.

(To Pseudartabas) Now come along! Tell me plainly in the face of this (Dicaeopolis brandishes his fist), or else I'll give you a bath of red Sardic dye. Is the Great King going to send us gold?

(Pseudartabas shakes his head).

Then we are being wantonly deceived by our ambassadors?

(Pseudartabas nods his head).

115   At any rate these fellows nod in good Greek. It's not impossible that they come from round here. And one of these two eunuchs I know: it's Sibyrtius' son,

120   Cleisthenes. You smooth, hot-tempered arse! With a beard like yours, have you come here got up as a eunuch, you ape? As for this one here, whoever is it? It isn't Straton, surely?

Crier:-   Silence! Sit down! The Council invites the King's Eye to the Town Hall (prytaneion).

125   Dicaeopolis:-   Well, isn't this enough to make you choke? And then I'm left hanging round here, but the door is never closed against their entertaining people. I'm going to do something really shocking. Where's Amphitheus?

Amphitheus:-   Here I am.

130   Dicaeopolis:-   Here are eight drachmas: take them and make a private peace with the Spartans for me and my children and my wife.

(To the rest of the Assembly) As for you, get on with your stupid embassies!

Crier:-   Theōrus, returning from an embassy to Sitalces, to come forward!

(enter Theōrus)

Theōrus:-   Here I am.

135   Dicaeopolis:-   Here's another charlatan being announced.

Theōrus:-   We should not have stayed so long in Thrace ....

Dicaeopolis:-   My God you wouldn't, if you hadn't been drawing good pay.

Theōrus:-   ....if snow hadn't fallen all over Thrace and frozen the rivers.

140   Dicaeopolis:-   That was the time when Theognis was such a frost in the festival here! (This playwright was in fact nicknamed 'Snow', because his poetry was so chilling).

Theōrus:-   I spent this time drinking with Sitalces. He really was extraordinarily pro-Athenian. He was such a true friend of yours that he even kept writing on the

145   walls "Long live the Athenians". And his son, whom we had made an Athenian citizen, was passionately fond of sausages from the Apaturia ceremony, and he

kept begging his father to send help to the fatherland. And his father took a
solemn oath to send such a great army that the Athenians would say, "What a
150 swarm of locusts is approaching".
Dicaeopolis:- I'm damned if I believe a word of what you just said, except
the bit about the locusts.
Theōrus:- And now he has sent you the best tribe of fighting men in Thrace.
Dicaeopolis:- Well, at least that's plain enough!
155 Crier:- Thracians who came with Theōrus, come forward! (Enter a throng
of Odomantians wearing artificial sex-organs of monstrous size).
Dicaeopolis:- What mischief have we here?

Theōrus:- An army of Odomantians.
Dicaeopolis:- Odomantians? What's this? Have any of the Odomantians
been circumcised?
160 Theōrus:- If anyone will give them two drachmas' pay, they will overrun the
whole of Boeotia.
Dicaeopolis:- Two drachmas a day for these filthy fellows? The thranite
sailors (i.e. those on the highest bench, pulling the longest oars), saviours
of our city, would belly-ache at that. (An Odomantian makes off with Dicaeopolis'
snack-lunch). Help! This is the end; plundered of my garlic-lunch by
165 Odomantians! Put my garlic down, won't you?
Theōrus (to the Odomantian):- You poor fool, don't go near them when they've
been primed with garlic.
Dicaeopolis:- You prytaneis, are you going to stand and watch me being maltreated
on my home ground - and by barbarous foreigners at that? I forbid you to put the
170 question of pay for the Thracians on the agenda. And I tell you that there's a sign
from heaven here: I've felt a drop of rain.
Crier:- The Thracians are to leave and come back on the day after tomorrow.
The prytaneis now dissolve the Assembly.

<u>Another Meeting of the Assembly</u>

Although this occasion is a hundred years later, the procedure is the
same.

<u>Demosthenes, On the Crown 169-170</u>

169 It was evening when a messenger came to the <u>prytaneis</u> to announce the capture of
Elateia (in 339). And after this some of them got up at once in the middle of
dinner and drove the men out of the tents in the <u>Agora</u> and set fire to the booths,
while others sent for the <u>Generals</u> (stratēgoi) and summoned the trumpeter. The
city was full of confusion. At dawn the next day the prytaneis called the Council
into the Council-chamber, while you citizens marched into the Assembly. In fact
before the Council had completed its business or drafted the <u>probouleuma</u>, the
170 whole <u>dēmos</u> was seated above. Next, when the Council had come in and the
prytaneis had announced the news which had been reported to them, and they had
brought in the messenger who had come and he had told his story, then the Crier
asked the question, "Who wishes to speak?" But nobody came forward. And
although the Crier asked his question a number of times, the result was no better:
nobody stood up to speak, even though every one of our Generals was there and
every one of our usual speakers (<u>rhētores</u>), and though our country was calling
with a united voice for a man to speak and show us the way to safety. For it is
right to regard the words that the Crier speaks in accordance with the laws as
the united voice of our country.

<u>A Mock Council</u>

The proceedings parodied are those of the Council when an impeachment
(<u>eisangelia</u>) on a treason charge came before it.

<u>Aristophanes, Knights 624-682</u>

625 Sausage-seller:- It's a story worth hearing. Listen! I rushed from here close

on Paphlagon's heels. He was already shaking up a storm inside the Council-
chamber, breaking off thunderous words and hurling them, however far-fetched,
at the Knights. He piled up his tall stories and called you conspirators (synōmotai)
630 - and made it all sound true. The whole Council was spiced with this growth of
lies as it listened to him, and gave a look like mustard, and knitted its brows.
When I saw the Council was taking in all he said, and was being tricked by his
impostures, I said to myself, "Come down, you guardian spirits of rascals and
635 quacks, gods of all fools, imps and impudent demons, and you, Agora, where
I was brought up as a boy, give me audacity, a glib tongue and a shameless
voice". As I prayed, I heard thunder on my right - coming from beneath
640 some dirty old man! I prostrated myself at this good omen; and then with a
firm butt of the buttocks, I burst open the gate (of the bar of the Council-chamber)
and stretching my jaws I shouted:- "O Council, I want to bring you first some
645 good news: Ever since war broke out, I have never seen sprats so cheap". At
once their ruffled faces were calmed, and I was voted a garland for my good
tidings. And making it a state-secret - for them - I added:- "To get lots of
650 sprats for one obol, you should quickly commandeer all the pots from the
craftsmen (thus paralysing the market in sprats). They applauded me, gaping
in admiration. But Paphlagon tumbled to my game - after all, he knows what
sort of talk pleases the Council best - and he made this proposal:- "My friends,
655 I am resolved to offer one hundred oxen in recognition of this most welcome news".
The Council veered back towards him. So when I saw I was being defeated by this
bullshit, I trumped his ace and cried, "Two hundred oxen", and I moved that a
660 vow be made to Artemis of a thousand goats, if anchovies weren't a hundred for
an obol by tomorrow. The Council craned their heads forward - towards me
again. When he heard this, Paphlagon in his amazement began to waffle and drivel
665 on - until the prytaneis and the Archers dragged him out. The Councillors stood
up and started to talk noisily about the sprats. But Paphlagon pleaded with them
to wait just a moment. "Hear what the Spartan envoy has to say. He comes
670 with proposals for a truce", he said. But with one voice the Councillors shouted
back:- "What? - a truce at a time like this? Just because the Spartans have
heard that sprats are cheap in Athens! You're a dead loss; we don't need peace.
Let the war drag on". They shouted for the prytaneis to close the session, and
675 then they leapt over the bar in every direction. But I took a short cut to the Agora,
and bought up all the coriander and leeks that were there, and when the Councillors
could find no seasoning for their sprats, I gave these to them for nothing. How
680 popular I was! They all made such a fuss of me, and praised me sky-high!
That's how I've come here with the whole Council in my pocket, all for an obol's
worth of coriander.

9. THE MYTILENE DEBATE

Mytilene revolted from the Athenian Empire in 428 and was reduced by
Paches in 427. He sent the ring-leaders to Athens and awaited orders
from the Assembly on how the city should be punished. Thucydides
puts into the mouths of Cleon and Diodotus the main arguments used in
the debate in the Assembly.

See Thucydides 3.36-38 (P. 180-182); 41-43 (P. 185-187); 49-50.1 (P. 190).

10. THE PYLOS DEBATES

After a truce had been arranged with the Generals at Pylos, a Spartan
embassy arrived at Athens to negotiate for peace (425). Thucydides
relates how Cleon persuaded the Athenians to demand unrealistic terms
- although later they began to regret not having made peace.

See Thucydides 4.21-22 (P. 241-242); 27.3-28 (P. 246-247).

11. DEMAGOGUES, DICASTS AND INFORMERS

The Demagogues

According to the poet, their characteristics are (a) ignorance; (b) a foul tongue and low birth; (c) ubiquity.

Aristophanes, Knights 190-194; 211-219; 303-313

190   Demosthenes:- That is your only handicap, your ability to read, however badly. For leadership of the dēmos (dēmagōgia) is no longer the job of a man who is cultured (mousikos) and respectable (chrēstos) in his behaviour, but of the uneducated (amathēs) and brutal. So don't waste what the gods in their oracles offer you.

211   Sausage-seller:- The words of the oracle flatter me; but I wonder how I can guide the dēmos.
  Demosthenes:- There's nothing to it; just carry on in your usual way.
215   Mangle and make mincemeat of everything, and win over the dēmos by always sweetening them with your cook-shop rhetoric. You've got all the other qualifications for a leader of the dēmos (dēmagōgos), a filthy voice, common birth and barrow-boy (agoraios) character, - yes, everything you need for statesmanship (politeia).

303   Chorus of Knights:- You vile and brutal brawler, your impudence has spread
305   throughout the land, throughout the Assembly, the government and lawsuits and
310   jury-courts, you mud-stirrer; you have shaken up our whole city, and deafened Athens with your shouts, watching like a tunny-fisher from the rocks above for tribute (phoros).

The Demagogue and the Jury-courts

Aristophanes, Knights 255-283

255   Paphlagon:- Old men of the Heliaea, members of the three-obol brotherhood, I take care of you, right or wrong, with my bawling; now come to my aid, for I am being attacked by conspirators (synōmotai).
  Chorus of Knights:- Deservedly too, because you gobble up public money before you are allotted your share, and with your eyes on those facing public scrutiny (hypeuthūnoi) you press and squeeze the 'grasses' (literally, figs), however
260   green or soft they may be, and if you see any man who is not active in public life (apragmōn) and gapes at you, then you recall him from Chersonese, slang him, bring him down by hook or by crook, twist his shoulder and end up by getting him with a pin-fall. And you see which of the citizens is a simpleton, and
265   rich and respectable (not ponēros) and shuddering at political involvement.
  Paphlagon:- Are you ganging up on me? Men, it is on your account that I am being attacked, because I was just going to propose that it is only fair to set up in the city a memorial to you for your bravery.
  Chorus:- What a charlatan, and a slippery character, too. Do you see how he
270   cringes before us as if we were old men. Look at the tricks he's up to. But if he gets the better of us on this side, we'll hit him on the other; and if he dodges in this direction, he'll only come charging into my boot there!
  Paphlagon:- O city, O dēmos, what savage beasts are punching me in the belly!
  Chorus:- And you've started bawling the way you usually do when you're causing an uproar in the city.
275   Paphlagon:- But I'll put you to flight with this shouting first.
  Chorus:- Well, if you do win the day with your shouting, you shall have the crown of victory. But if the sausage-seller outdoes you in impudence, the prize is ours.
  Paphlagon:- I'm going to lay information against this man: I say that he fits out the Spartan triremes with - soup.
280   Sausage-seller:- Yes, and I denounce Paphlagon too, because when he trots down with an empty stomach to the Town Hall (prytaneion), he's full up when he runs home again!
  Demosthenes:- Yes, loaded with forbidden loot - bread and meat and fish-fillet; Pericles was never rewarded so.

The Demagogues as Warmongers

Aristophanes, Peace 632-648, (produced in 421)

Hermes:- Then when the working population flocked in from the country, they
did not realise that they were being sold in the same way (as the allied cities
had been), but since they were without grapes and were fond of figs, they looked
635 to the public speakers.   But these speakers were well aware that the poor farmers
were weak and short of barley, and drove away this goddess (Peace) with pitch-
forked screams, though through her fondness for this land she had often manifested
herself;   they also shook up any of the allies who were fat and rich, by bringing
640 forward accusations that they were supporting Brasidas.   Then, like a pack of
puppies, you tore the victim to shreds;   for the city turned pale and sat in fear,
and gladly swallowed all the slanders anyone cast before it.   And when the allies
645 saw the blows they were suffering, they began to stuff gold into the mouths of the
men who were causing this, thereby making them rich, while Greece was milked
dry, and you didn't even notice.   The man who did all this was a tanner (i.e. Cleon).

Love of Litigation

The Athenian love of litigation is attacked in many of the plays of
Aristophanes, particularly in the Wasps (produced in 422) from which
the following passages are taken.   It is often evident that the poet is
not unsympathetic to the jurymen (dicasts) themselves, but is a bitter
opponent of the unscrupulous attempts of the demagogues to exploit them.

Aristophanes, Wasps 85-135

85 Xanthias:- Absolute nonsense.   You'll never guess;   but if you really want to
know, listen quietly and I will tell you what disease our master suffers from.   He
loves the Heliaea, as no man ever has.   He loves it, this dicast business;   and
90 he groans if he can't sit on the front bench.   He doesn't get even a wink of sleep
at night, but if in fact he does doze off just for a moment, his mind still flies
through the night to the water-clock (clepsydra).   And because he's so used to
95 holding the voting-pebble, he gets up holding three of his fingers together, as if
he's offering frankincense at the new moon.   And by God, if he saw any scribbling
on the doorway, "Pretty Dēmos, son of Pyrilampes", he would go and write by
100 the side, "Pretty Ballot-box".   And he said that the cock which used to crow
from evening-time, woke him up too late because it had been won over and bribed
by officials under investigation (hypeuthūnoi).   Straight after supper he shouts
for his shoes, and then off he goes to the court in the early hours and sleeps
105 there, clinging to the column like a limpet.   And through bad temper he awards
the long line (i.e. the severer penalty) to all the defendants, and then comes home
like a bee or bumble-bee, with wax plastered under his finger-nails.   And because
110 he's afraid that some day he may run short of pebbles for voting with, he keeps
a whole beach in his house.   That's how mad he is.   And if anyone ever gives
him any advice, he plays the dicast all the more.   So we're keeping guard on
him: we've tied him up and bolted him in, so that he won't escape.   For his
115 son is angry at this illness of his.   At first he tried to console him with words
and to persuade him not to put on his ragged cloak and go out;   but he would not
obey.   Then his son washed him and cleaned him up;   but he still wouldn't obey.
After this, he tried to purify him with Corybantic rites, but his father dashed out,
120 kettle-drum and all, and rushed into the New Court and began to play the dicast.
Then when his son didn't achieve anything by these rites, he sailed over to Aegina,
and then seized his father and made him sleep the night in the temple of Asclepius -
125 but he still turned up at the bar of the court at dawn!   Since then we've never let
him out, but he's taken to slipping away down the drainpipes or through the sky-
lights.   We stuffed rags into all the openings there were and blocked them up,
130 but like a jackdaw he hammered pegs into the wall for himself, and then out he
hopped.   So we've spread nets over the whole yard and we're keeping guard all
round.   The old man's name is Philocleon (Cleon-lover), and his son here is
135 Bdelycleon (Cleon-hater), quite an arrogant and haughty character.

11

The Jury-courts (dicastēria)

Four places of business are mentioned and show how widespread were the dicasts activities. The Chorus of Wasps represents Philocleon's fellow-dicasts.

Aristophanes, Wasps 1102-1121

Chorus of Wasps:- If you consider us in our many spheres of action, you will find us in all ways very wasp-like in our habits and way of life. In the first
1105 place, no creature when provoked is more sharp-tempered or cross than we; then we manage all our business in a waspish fashion. We gather in swarms and, like wasps' nests, some of us serve as dicasts where the archon summons us, others with the Eleven, some in the Odeion, and others by the city walls,
1110 huddled closely together, bowing to the ground, scarcely moving, like grubs in the cell of the combs. But in the rest of our way of life we are full of resource; for we sting everyone and that's how we get our livelihood. Yet
1115 we have stingless drones sitting among us, who stay at home and eat up the fruit of our labours, doing no hard work themselves. But what we find most painful is if someone who has never seen military service, nor held an oar or a spear or got a blister for this land's sake, swallows up our pay. In short,
1120 I think that in future any citizen who has no sting should not get the three obols.

Attractions of the Dicast's Life

Philocleon sets out to prove how great is the power held by the dicast and in so doing enumerates the attractions of a dicast's life.

Aristophanes, Wasps 548-612

Philocleon:- Well then, beginning as soon as we leave the starting posts, I will
550 prove to you that no king has power superior to ours. For what is there in existence more fortunate and more blessed than a juryman? Is there any creature more pampered or cleverer, and that too even when he is old? First, when I crawl out of bed in the morning there are watching for me at the bar of the court great six-foot fellows; and then as soon as I approach, one slips his delicate hand into mine, his hand that has stolen from the public funds;
555 they bow and beseech me, pouring forth piteous words: "Have mercy on me, father, I beg you, if you yourself ever pilfered when holding office or when buying for your mess-mates on a campaign." And he would never have known of my existence but for his previous acquittal.
Bdelycleon:- Let me make a note here about these people pleading with you.
560 Philocleon:- Then once I'm inside the court after listening to their pleas, with my anger all wiped away, I do none of these things that I've promised. But I listen to them uttering all sorts of words designed to obtain acquittal. Now let me see! What flattery can one not hear there, addressed to a juryman?
565 Some bewail their poverty and exaggerate their misfortunes until, in the end, they make them out to be equal to - mine. Others tell us tales, some try a comic fable of Aesop's, others crack jokes, to make me laugh and lose my anger, and if we are not persuaded by these devices, the defendant leads in his small
570 children, his girls and his boys, by the hand, and I listen. They huddle together and bleat like lambs; and then, trembling, the father on their behalf beseeches me, as if I were a god, to acquit him and pass his accounts (euthūna): "If you love the bleating of a lamb, hear with pity my boy; or if you delight in piglets, listen to my daughter." And we then slightly relax the tension of our anger.
575 Oh, is this not a great office, that quite puts riches in the shade?
Bdelycleon:- Now I write this second note about you: 'This office puts riches in the shade'. And now relate to me the advantages that you have, to support your claim that you rule Hellas.
Philocleon:- It is one of our duties to look at the private parts of young men when they are registered (dokimasia) in the rolls of adult citizens. And if Oeagrus comes to court to plead, he is not acquitted until he recites for us
580 his best speech from the 'Niobe'. And if a flute-player wins his case, as a

-24-

payment for acquittal he pipes a march - wea Ir.g the mouthband and producing
his sweetest tone - for the jurymen as they leave the court.   And if a father
leaves an heiress daughter and on his deathbed entrusts her to someone, we say
585   that the will and the cap that sits so solemnly on the seals can go to pot, and we give
her to the man who persuades us by his pleas.   And this we do without having to
render an account (anhypeuthūnoi).   But no other office has such unfettered power.
Bdelycleon:- Truly grand, but only in this one respect do I call you fortunate.
Yet you are wrong to open the seal on a will about an heiress.
590   Philocleon:- And if ever the Council or the Assembly of the dēmos cannot reach
a decision in judging some weighty matter, they pass a vote that the wrongdoers
are to be handed over to the jurymen;   then Euathlus and this great toady
Cleonymus who threw away his shield declare that they will never betray us, but
will always fight for the plēthos.   And nobody ever gets a measure passed before
595   the dēmos, unless he proposes that the jury-courts should be discharged as soon
as they have given one verdict;   and Cleon himself, that great tub-thumper, is
the only one who does not carp at us, but sets his hand to the job of protecting us
and waves away the flies for us.   You never did a single one of these things for
your very own father.   But although Theōrus is a man as important as Euphēmius,
600   even he blacks our shoes with a sponge from the jar.   Consider of what great
advantages you deprive me and rob me;   and yet you said you would prove that
this power of mine is mere slavery and menial work.
Bdelycleon:- Have your fill of chattering.   You will stop some time and then I
will show that, in this matter of your vaunted office, you are just an old left-over
that nobody bothers to clear away.
605   Philocleon:- But the sweetest pleasure of all, which I forgot to mention, is when
I go home with my pay;   and then when I come in, everyone welcomes me because
of the money.   First my daughter washes me and anoints my feet and hangs over
me and kisses me, and while she calls me "Dear Daddy", she winkles out my
610   three obols.   And my wife pets me and brings me a barley scone, and then as
she sits beside me, urges me, "Eat this", and "Get your teeth into that".

    This pay for attendance at the jury-courts was an important source of
    income to needier Athenians.

Aristophanes, Wasps 303-311

Boy:- Well then, father, if the archon is not holding a sitting of the jury-court
305   now, how shall we buy any lunch?   Have you some hopeful plan for us, or some
means..... (he continues, singing a well-known line) "some sacred means of
crossing Helle".
310   Chorus:- Woe is me!   Alas, woe, woe!   No, I don't know where our next meal
is coming from.

The Dicast Disillusioned

    Bdelycleon replies that, whereas the dicasts think themselves masters of
    everyone, they are in fact slaves of the demagogues.

Aristophanes, Wasps 655-724

655   Bdelycleon:- Now listen, Daddy darling, and relax your stern expression a little.
First reckon roughly, not in exact figures, but in round numbers, the tribute
(phoros) that we receive altogether from the allied cities;   and in addition to
this, reckon the dues (telē) and all the 1% duties, the court fees (prytaneia),
the dues on mines, markets (agorai) and harbours, the rents, and the public
660   sales.   The sum of these brings us somewhere near 2,000 talents.   From all
this now put aside the annual pay for the jurymen, 6,000 of them, and the total
has never yet been larger: 150 talents a year, I suppose, is what it costs us.
Philocleon:- Then our pay is not even one tenth of the revenue.
665   Bdelycleon:- That is perfectly true.
Philocleon:- And what becomes of all the rest of the revenue?

Bdelycleon:- It goes to those who 'will never betray the rowdy Athenian mob (kolosyrtos), but will always fight for the plēthos,' because you, father, are taken in by their rhetoric and choose them to rule over you. And they take
670 bribes from the allied cities, 50 talents or so, threatening them and frightening them with words like these: "You will pay your tribute (phoros) or I will come thundering and will overthrow your city". And yet you are content with nibbling away at the remnants and shreds of your own power. But when the allies see the rest, the dregs, wasting away at the voting-urn and eating nothing, they
675 think you are not worth more than a pauper's vote, and so it is to these (demagogues) that they bring their presents: jars of pickles, wine, rugs, cheese, honey, sesame seeds, pillows, bowls, woollen cloaks, wreaths, necklaces, beakers, health and wealth. But to you, you who have toiled so much on land and sea, from all that you control nobody gives you so much as a head of garlic to flavour your boiled sprats.
680 **Philocleon:-** That's true, for, by Zeus, I sent out just now for three heads of garlic from the greengrocer myself. But you're wearing me out by being so slow in proving this slavery of mine.
Bdelycleon:- Well, is it not pure slavery that all these men are in office, and their hangers-on too, earning pay, and yet if anyone gives you your three obols, you are full of gratitude? - obols which you won yourself with a lot of hard toil
685 whilst rowing in the navy, serving with the infantry, and taking part in sieges. And in addition to this, - and this makes me choke with rage - you come constantly, under orders, whenever some young whipper-snapper, some son of Chaereas, comes forward, straddling his legs, swaying his body, with mincing airs, and orders you to be punctual and be in your seats on time, because if any of you
690 comes after the signal, he will not be paid his three obols. But he carries off his drachma, his fee as counsel for the prosecution, even if he does arrive late. Then if any of the defendants gives him a bribe, which he shares with a colleague in office, they hurry to arrange the matter between them, like men
695 sawing, one pulling, the other giving way; while you gape at the Treasurer (kōlakretēs) and never notice what is happening.
Philocleon:- Is that what they do to me? Oh, what are you saying? You disturb me to the depths of my being, you undermine my ideas, and I do not know what you are doing to me.
Bdelycleon:- Consider then, when it is possible for you and all your fellows to be rich, how you have somehow been hedged in by all these 'people's men'.
700 You who rule most of the cities from Pontus to Sardis enjoy nothing, not so much as a scrap, except what you earn. And even this they dole out to you in drops, like oil from wool, just enough to keep you alive. For they want you to be poor, and I will tell you why: so that you may recognise your keeper. And then
705 whenever he hisses at you, urging you against one of his enemies, you will spring fiercely to the attack. For if they wanted to provide a livelihood for the dēmos, it would be easy. There are at least 1000 cities that now pay tribute (phoros) to us; if anyone commanded each of these to feed twenty men, 20,000 of the ordinary citizens (of Athens) would be living in luxury, with
710 garlands of all sorts, and the freshest milk and creamy puddings, enjoying things worthy of this land and of the trophy won at Marathon. But as it is, you're like olive-pickers, following after the man who hands out your pay.
Philocleon:- Alas, what is this numbness that steals over my hand? I cannot even hold my sword; I'm feeling weak now.
715 **Bdelycleon:-** But whenever these officials are afraid, they are ready to give you Euboea and promise to supply corn, 50 bushels for every man; but they never yet actually gave you any, except 5 bushels just recently - and this you received
718 doled out by the quart, only after you had had a lot of trouble proving your citizenship. That's the reason why I always kept you shut inside the house,
720 because I wanted to look after you, and didn't want these men with their empty vauntings to laugh at you. And now my entire wish is to provide what you want, except only a draught of Treasurer's (kōlakretēs) milk.

Informers

Athens had no standing public prosecutors and Solon's legislation
permitted anyone to prosecute wrongdoers. The system worked well
at first, but by c.450 a class of professional prosecutors had grown up.
These were called sycophants and often prosecuted for political motives
and private profit. The most obnoxious practice that they employed
was blackmail. But despite the abuses to which it became subject,
Solon's law was never repealed, so fundamental was it held to be to
the democracy.

Aristotle, Constitution of Athens 9.1

The three most democratic features of Solon's constitution seem to be these:-
First and foremost, that no one shall lend money on the security of a person's
body; secondly, that anyone "who wishes" to do so may assist the victims of
wrongdoing to obtain redress; thirdly, and this is generally said to have
resulted in political power for the plethos, the right of appeal to the jurycourt.

Although the Plutus is a late play of Aristophanes (388), the behaviour
of its informer is typical of his fifth-century predecessor. For scenes
involving informers in earlier plays, see Birds 1410-1468 and Acharnians
908-958.

Aristophanes, Plutus 899-934

900 Informer:- How I suffer for being respectable (chrēstos) ! What trouble my
patriotism brings!
Just Man:-   You - patriotic and respectable?
Informer:-   There's no one to touch me.
Just Man:- Now answer this question.
Informer:- Well then?
Just Man:- Are you a farmer?
Informer:- Do I seem so sour?
Just Man:- A merchant then?
Informer:- Yes - at any rate I diddle people when it suits me!
905 Just Man:- Well, have you learnt a trade?
Informer:- Good Lord, no.
Just Man:- How have you managed to live without doing anything?
Informer:- I am superintendant of all public and private business.
Just Man:- You? What qualifications have you?
Informer:- I am the man "who wishes".
Just Man:- How then could you be respectable (chrēstos), you crook, when
910 nothing is your concern and everybody hates you?
Informer:- Isn't it my concern to benefit my own city, you twit, to the utmost
of my power?
Just Man:- Does meddling (polypragmosynē) benefit the city?
Informer:- No, but coming to the rescue of the established laws does, and
915 not allowing anyone to violate them.
Just Man:- Doesn't the city appoint jurymen to office for this very purpose?
Informer:- But who prosecutes?
Just Man:- Any man "who wishes".
Informer:- That's who I am, and so the city's business is my concern.
920 Just Man:- Good Lord, what a worthless (ponēros) champion (prostatēs) the city
has. Why don't you be the man "who wishes" to keep quiet and lead a life of ease?
Informer:- But that's a sheep's life with nothing to do.
Just Man:- So you wouldn't learn a new trade?
925 Informer:- Not even if you gave me Plutus (Wealth) himself and Battus' silphium.
Just Man:-   Quick, take your cloak off.
Cario (a slave):- You there, he's speaking to you.
Just Man:- Now untie your shoes.

Cario:- This all applies to you.

Informer:- Let one of you "who wishes" come near me!

Cario:- Then I'm your man.

930 Informer:- Oh dear, help! I'm being stripped in broad daylight.

Cario:- Yes, because you choose to live by meddling in other people's business.

Informer:- Do you realise what you're doing? I appeal for a witness.

Just Man:- Your witness has just left in a hurry.

Informer:- Help! I've been deserted - I'm trapped!

12.   THE OLD OLIGARCH

The Old Oligarch I; II; III, 1-9, 12-13

See the Introduction and Translation in LACTOR 2, The Old Oligarch.

13.   THE NEW EDUCATION: THE SOPHISTS AND SOCRATES

Before the rise of the Sophistic movement in the fifth century Athens had only the most elementary education to offer her citizens.   The Sophists filled the need, created by the rise of the democracy, for an intellectual training to fit a man for service in the Assembly and the jurycourts.   It was at Athens, the intellectual centre of Greece, that the Sophists conducted most of their teaching.   Even in the fifth century they charged high fees, and it was therefore the richer class who had the time and money to avail themselves of this type of education.   It is easy to understand how to democratic eyes the Sophists' teaching came to appear partisan, for from the ranks of their pupils came the leaders of the oligarchs.   (See, e.g., Thucydides 8, 68 (P. 526)).
The Clouds was produced in 423: in these passages (written some years later for a revised version), Aristophanes contrasts the hardy simplicity and good manners of olden times with the new intellectualism.

The Old Teaching

Aristophanes, Clouds 961-1008

Just Argument:- So now I'll explain the old educational system of the days when I flourished through advocating justice when moderation (sōphrosynē) was the regular thing.   In the first place, boys were seen and not heard; secondly,

965 our fellow-villagers used to walk in the streets in an orderly fashion on their way to the harp-teacher's house, all keeping together, and lightly-clad even if there was a blanket of snow on the ground.   Then again they used to learn off by heart a chant, either "Terrible Pallas, sacker of cities", or "Some far-ranging shout".   They didn't sit cross-legged, but raised high the traditional tune handed down from their fathers.   And if one of them should sink so low

970 as to make a sudden trill in it, like the intricate flourishes introduced by Phrynis' followers nowadays, he would be punished and beaten severely, for darkening the reputation of the Muses.   The boys had to keep their thighs covered up when sitting in the wrestling-teachers school, so as to show nothing indecent to

975 passers-by; then again, when they got up, they had to smoothe out the sand and take care not to leave an impression for the lovers of youth.   In those days no boy annointed himself below the navel, and so the first downy hair on his genitals bloomed as on a fruit.   Nor would he go to a lover, putting on a soft voice or flashing his eyes to flaunt his attractions; nor could he take even a head of

980 radish at dinner, or snatch any dill or celery from the older men, or live on dainty dishes, or giggle, or cross his legs at the table.

Unjust Argument:- What quaint ideas - a hangover from the Dipolieia,

985 choc-a-bloc with cicadas and Kekeides and the Bouphonia!

Just Argument:- But all the same, my system of education was based on this ancient discipline, and it provided the veterans of Marathon with their upbringing. But you teach modern man from birth to wrap himself up in a cloak; so it chokes

990 me when one of the men who are there to dance at the Panathenaea holds up his
shield, reveals all, and quite forgets Athena, the Triton-born. So, young man,
choose me with confidence as the "Stronger Argument", and you will learn a few
lessons - how to hate the Agora, stay away from the baths, be ashamed at what is
shameful, and be angry if anyone laughs at you; and to stand up when your elders
995 approach, and not be rude to your parents, and do nothing else that is shameful,
because you want to form an image of modesty in your heart; and not to rush into
any dancing-girl's house - otherwise, as you're gawking at her, the tart may
hit you with her melons and your reputation will be shattered; and not to argue
with your father, or hold his age against him by calling him Iapetus, when it was
he who raised you from the day you were hatched.
1000 Unjust Argument:- Good Heavens, if you take any notice of this, young man, you
will be called a Mummy's boy, just like the sons of Hippocrates.
Just Argument:- But then at least you'll pass the time in the Gymnasia, looking
sleek and fresh, instead of making crude jokes in the Agora, like the present
generation, or being dragged into the courts on some hair-splitting-pettifogging-
1005 barefaced- good-for-nothing issue; no, you'll go to the Academy with a sensible
(sōphrōn) young friend, and, wearing a garland of white reed, will run races
under the sacred olive trees. You'll be fragrant with honeysuckle and the quiet
life (apragmosynē) and the lime-tree, and rejoice in the season of spring, when
the plane-tree whispers to the elm.

The New Teaching

Aristophanes, Clouds 1036-1062

Unjust Argument:- I've been bursting for ages with the desire to overthrow
all these ideas. The philosophers have called me the "Weaker Argument",
1040 simply because I was the very first to devise a way of speaking out as an opponent
of law and justice. It is worth more than any number of staters to choose the
weaker arguments and still win. But watch me now expose the educational system
(paideusis) he believes in - the system which first of all forbids you to have a hot
1045 bath. And yet by what reasoning do you find fault with hot baths?
Just Argument:- Because it is altogether evil, and makes a man a coward.
Unjust Argument:- Wait! It hasn't taken me long to get a hold on your waist;
you won't escape from this. Tell me, which of the sons of Zeus do you consider
was the bravest soul and suffered the most labours?
1050 Just Argument:- I think none surpasses Heracles.
Unjust Argument:- Well, have you ever seen cold water at Heracles' baths (at
Thermopylae)? Yet who was braver than him?
Just Argument:- It's because of arguments like this that the baths are full of
young men nattering all day long, while the wrestling-schools are empty.
1055 Unjust Argument:- Next, you criticise those who spend time in the Agora;
but I approve. If it had been a common (ponēros) activity, Homer would
never have made Nestor an orator in the Agora, nor all the other wise men.
And that brings me to the subject of the tongue, which he says young men shouldn't
1060 use, while I say they should. Again, he says they should act with moderation
(sōphrosynē): silence and moderation, the two worst qualities! I mean, tell
me who you have ever seen benefit from moderation, and prove me wrong by what
you say.

The Sophists

Protagoras of Abdera was born about 485 and spent his long life as one of
the most successful of the early sophists, teaching mainly at Athens.
His high repute won him the appointment as legislator of the new colony
at Thurii in 444. He was the first to accept fees for his teaching. The sophists
did not, of course, confine their teaching to political excellence (aretē),
which is the subject here. The jibe at Hippias below shows well the
breadth of their interests.

Plato, Protagoras 318 D - 320 B

318 D   And Protagoras, hearing me say this, replied:- "That's a good question of
yours, Socrates, and for my part I enjoy answering good questions. When
Hippocrates becomes my pupil he will not find happening to him what he would
have found if he had become a pupil of any other sophist.   All the others

E   maltreat their young men, who have no sooner escaped from the acquisition
of special skills (technai) than they are reluctantly forced back to a further
dose of them and to the study of arithmetic or astronomy or geometry or
music (mousikē)" - with this he gave Hippias a look - "but when Hippocrates
comes to me, he will learn only what he came to learn, firstly wisdom (euboulia)

319 A   in family matters and the best way to run his own household, and secondly wisdom
in public affairs and the way to become as competent (dunatos) as possible in public
action and public speaking".
  "I wonder if I follow you" I said, "You seem to me to be talking of a special
political skill (technē) and to be promising to make men good citizens."
  "You've got it Socrates.   That is precisely my prospectus."
  "Well", I said, "in that case you have indeed got hold of a fine skill to impart.
But - for to you of all men I mean to be entirely frank - have you got hold of this
skill? I had supposed, Protagoras, that this was not a teachable subject: yet

B   when you say it is, I don't see how I can disbelieve you.   The right course will be
for me to tell you why I do not think it is teachable nor something which can be
provided by one man for another. Well, I, like the rest of Greece, regard the
Athenians as clever.   Now at our meetings of the Assembly I observe that
when the Athenians have to take a decision about a building matter, it is the
builders they summon to give advice about the buildings, and if the decision is
about ship-building, they summon the ship-builders, and so likewise in all
matters involving what they regard as teachable skills, they summon the expert:

C   and if someone tries to advise them whom they do not regard as a professional
craftsman, no matter how handsome or rich he is or how noble (gennaios) his
family, they won't listen to him, but jeer at him and boo him, until the would-be
speaker either gives way to the 'boos' and stands down of his own accord or else
is dragged or carried off by the Archers on the orders of the prytaneis.   So
much for the Athenians' handling of what they regard as technical matters.

D   But when it comes to a decision about the running of the city, then you will
find standing up to advise them carpenter, smith, cobbler, merchant, ship's
captain, rich man, poor man, noble (gennaios) or low-born (agennēs) all alike,
and this time nobody reproaches them with trying to give advice without a basis
of expert knowledge and instruction - obviously on the assumption that there is

E   no teachable kind of skill involved.   And the same truth which is apparent in
our politics holds good in our private affairs as well.   The cleverest and best
of our citizens are unable to pass on their aretē to others.   You have only to
look at Pericles, these young lads' father.   In all matters which come within
the province of teachers, he gave them an excellent education (paideia), but

320 A   in those matters where his own special ability (sophia) lies he neither educates
them himself nor entrusts anyone else with the task: they simply go around
on their own like grazing sheep and pick up what they can in the way of aretē.
Or, if you like, take the case of Kleinias, the younger brother of Alcibiades
here.   This same Pericles was his guardian and, fearing no doubt that
Alcibiades might corrupt him, he took him away and put him in Ariphron's
household to be educated: then, before six months were up, he restored him

B   to Alcibiades, not knowing what on earth to do with him.   I could give you plenty
of other examples of men who were good themselves but never made anyone
else better either of their own family or another's.   And so, Protagoras, with
all this in mind, I cannot regard aretē as a teachable thing.   Yet, when I hear
your claims, I find myself wavering and thinking there must be something in
what you say, regarding you as I do as a man of much experience and much
learning - with some original discoveries to your credit too".

Democratic Hostility towards the Sophistic ＿ᴖlitical Education

Plato, Meno 90 E - 92 B

90 E
91 A
Socrates:- Quite right. Now you can join me in considering the case of our foreign friend here, Meno. He has been telling me for a long time, Anytus, of his longing for this kind of cleverness (<u>sophia</u>) and <u>aretē</u> which enables men to run their household or city well, to look after their parents and to know how to entertain fellow-citizens or foreigners as a good man should. So consider to

B whom we should send him to acquire this aretē. Our recent conversation suggests, doesn't it, that the obvious men are these who claim to teach aretē and who make themselves available to any Greek who wants to learn from them, for a prearranged fee.

Anytus:- Whom do you mean, Socrates?

Socrates:- You must know as well as I do that I mean the men known as sophists.

C **Anytus:-** In heaven's name, hush, Socrates! I hope that at any rate none of my family or friends, citizen or foreigner, will fall victim to this mad craze of going to these men to be ruined: for ruination and corruption they manifestly are to their pupils.

Socrates:- Really, Anytus? Are these men unique then among those who claim to know how to benefit their pupils? Are they the only ones who not merely fail to help those entrusted to them, which is usual enough, but actually corrupt

D them? And do they blatantly make a charge for the privilege? I really cannot believe you. I know that Protagoras by himself made more money by this skill (sophia) than Pheidias with all his superbly lovely works and ten other sculptors put together. Your notion is too much to swallow. Shoe-menders or repairers

E of old garments couldn't get away with it for a month if they returned shoes and garments in a worse condition (<u>mochthērotera</u>) than when they received them, but would soon starve to death: yet you're asking me to believe that Protagoras managed to hide from the whole of Greece the fact that he was corrupting his pupils and sending them away worse (mochthēroteroi) than when he took them on, and got away with it for forty years, – I believe he was about seventy years old when he died and had been at his trade (technē) for forty of them, – so that all this time to this very day he has maintained a high reputation - and not only

92 A Protagoras but lots of others, some born before him but some still alive. Can we really say, as you do, that they deliberately deceived and ruined the young men? Or did they themselves not know what they were doing? In either case can we suppose they were so mad, these men who have been called by some the cleverest of mortals?

Anytus:- They are far from mad, Socrates. It is not they but much rather the young men who offer them money who are mad, and even madder are the

B relatives who entrust their young to these men, and maddest of all the cities which allow them in, instead of kicking out any foreigner peddling such a scheme - or citizen, for that matter.

Socrates

Socrates was a citizen of Athens who was born about 469 and executed in 399. He spent his life going out among his fellow citizens trying to make them better men. He himself wrote nothing, but a number of works written about him by his pupils survive, and of these the most important are Plato's dialogues.

To the average democrat Socrates would appear as just another Sophist, a teacher of young and dangerous oligarchs. Although such men as Alcibiades were his friends and pupils, he differed from their other teachers in that he took no fees and did not teach the rhetoric with which the sophists sought to give their pupils power in their cities. This he held to be no true knowledge but merely a valueless species of flattery. Socrates here maintains that he is the only true politician (in the proper sense of the word) in Athens, being the only man prepared to say what is best for the city and its people instead of the welcome flattery in which the other speakers indulge. Cf. Aristophanes, Acharnians 628-658 (p. 15f.)

Plato, Gorgias 521 D - 522 E

521 D   Socrates:- I think that few, if any other Athenians apart from myself essay the true political art (techne) and that I am the only politician alive. Being therefore a man who frames all his remarks without an eye to winning popularity,

E   aiming always at the best not the pleasantest course and refusing to indulge in the clever tricks you recommend, I shall have nothing to say in court. The same analogy occurs to me now as I used to Pōlus. I shall be brought to trial in similar circumstances to those of a doctor charged before a jury of children by a confectioner. What defence could a doctor in this predicament offer, if the prosecutor's charge ran as follows:- 'Children, this fellow has done you all much harm and is ruining and reducing to desperation the youngest among

522 A   you with his surgery and cauterizing and dieting and stifling, giving his bitter draughts and his regimes of hunger and thirst - how different from me, who regale you with many and manifold delights?' What could the poor doctor reply? If he told the truth and said 'Yes, I did all this, children, for your health', you can imagine the outcry from the jury in question.
Callicles:- Yes, probably there would be a big outcry.

B   Socrates:- And wouldn't our doctor be baffled what to say?
Callicles:- Yes, indeed.
Socrates:- Well, this would be exactly my predicament, if I was brought to court. I could recount no delights which I had provided for the jury - for the provision of delights is what they regard as beneficial service, though I myself envy neither the donors nor the recipients - and, if anyone accuses me of ruining the young men by reducing them to perplexity or of insulting the older men by my bitter words in private or in public, I shall be able to say neither the truth,

C   namely 'I do all this with justice: in fact I observe justice just as you swear to do in your oath, gentlemen', nor anything else: so probably I shall suffer whatever fate awaits me.
Callicles:- Do you think then, Socrates, that all is well with a man who finds himself in this predicament in his city and cannot provide any self-help?
Socrates:- I must suppose one thing, Callicles, which you have often granted.

D   I must suppose that self-help has taken the form of saying and doing nothing wrong in dealings with men or gods - the form of self-help we have often agreed to be the best. If someone accused me of being unable to give this form of help either to myself or to another, I should be ashamed before a tribunal of many or few or my own conscience, and if it was this sort of inability which brought me to my death, I should be unhappy. But if it were to be through lack of flattering rhetoric that I met my end, I am sure you would see me bear death

E   lightly. For no one who is not utterly irrational and unmanly is afraid of death itself but afraid, rather, of doing wrong. To arrive in Hades with a soul full of sins - that is the ultimate of all evils.

Socrates on the Citizen's Duties and his Debt to the City

Plato, Crito 50 C - 53 A

50 C   Socrates:- What then if the laws of Athens were to say to me, 'Come now,
D   Socrates! .... What have you got against us and the city, that you try to destroy us? Did we not in the first place give you birth and was it not through us that your father took your mother and begat you? Say then if you have some criticism of those laws among us which deal with marriage'. 'I have no criticism', I would say. 'Well, what of the laws which deal with the upbringing of a man after he is born and with his education (paideia) - the education which you, like others, have received? Did not those among us who are concerned with this lay down good ordinances in telling your father to educate you in music (mousike) and physical training (gymnastike)? 'They did,' I

. E   would say. 'Very well. After you were born and brought up and educated, could you in the first place claim that you were not our offspring and our slave - yourself and your forebears? And secondly, if this is so, do you think that you

-32-

and we have equal rights and that whatever we try to do to you, you have an
equal right to try to do back to us? Or are you suggesting that in relation
to your father, or to your master if you had one, you did not have equal rights,
entitling you to retaliate for what was done to you - to talk back when criticized

51 A and strike back when struck and so on; whereas in relation to your country,
apparently, and the laws, you are to be allowed this right of retaliation? If
we try to put an end to you, thinking this to be right, are you for your part
to retaliate by trying to put an end to us laws and the city as far you are able,
and to claim that in so doing you are acting justly, you who in truth care so
much for virtue (aretē) ? Or are you so clever that you have failed to notice
that, compared with your father and your mother and all your ancestors put

B together, your fatherland is a more precious and more venerable and more holy thing
and of more import to the gods and any thoughtful men, - more to be revered and
obeyed and humoured when angry than any father? Have you not realized that,
if dissuasion fails, you should do what your fatherland commands, and endure
without further demur any suffering it enjoins? Whether it be stripes or prison
or a call to be wounded or killed in war, - whatever the orders, they must be obeyed:
and this is the right of the matter: there must be no yielding or retreating or
desertion of one's post, but in war, in the jury-courts, and everywhere one must do

C what the city and the fatherland command or else persuade it that justice decrees
otherwise: for if the use of force against a mother or a father is sacrilege,
how much the more so is its use against one's fatherland!.' What reply shall
we make, Crito? That the laws are telling the truth or not?
Crito:- I think they are.
Socrates:- 'You must realize then, Socrates', the laws might continue, 'that if
we are speaking the truth, your present attempt against us is not right. For
after giving you birth and bringing you up and educating you and giving you and

D all your fellow-citizens a share in all the benefits we could, none the less by our
giving the necessary permission (exousia) we make public pronouncement that any
Athenian who wishes, once he is registered (dokimasia) as an adult citizen and has
seen for himself the politics of the city and us laws, may, if we do not please him,
take his possessions and remove to wherever he chooses. And none of us laws
stands in the way or forbids this, but whether in distaste for ourselves and the
city one of you chooses to go off to a colony, or he decides to migrate elsewhere,
we let him go where he wants with his possessions. But whoever among you

E remains when well aware of our methods of conducting lawsuits and of other
aspects of city administration, such a man we claim has by his action already
made a contract with us to do whatever we command. And if a man does not
thereafter obey us, we indict him under three heads: first that we, whom he
disobeys, are his parents, secondly that we are his nurses, thirdly that, after
agreeing to obey us, he does not do so nor seeks to persuade us of our errors,

52 A if there are any, - and this though we make a fair proposal and no harsh demand
that he shall do what we say, offering as we do alternatives, either dissuasion or
compliance, both of which he rejects. To these charges we claim that you too,
Socrates, will be liable, if you persist in doing what you have in mind, and you
especially of all the citizens of Athens.' And if I said, 'Why do you say that?'
they might justly reproach me with having entered into this contract more

B emphatically than any other Athenian. 'Socrates', they would say, 'we have
weighty evidence that we and the city have pleased you, since you would not
have lived in it so especially more than the others, had it not especially pleased
you. You have never left the city to go to the public games, except once to
the Isthmus, or to go anywhere else except on campaign. You have never been
abroad like other men nor shown any desire to know another city or other laws,

C but we and our city sufficed you, so emphatically did you choose us and agree
to be a citizen under us. You have even begotten children in Athens which
proves that it pleased you. What is more, during the trial itself you were
free to propose exile as your punishment if you wished, and what you are now

trying to do against the wishes of the city you could then have done with its approval. But what did you do? During the trial you put on a noble front of indifference to death and preferred, so you said, death to exile: now you show no shame before these words nor any regard for us laws whom you seek
D to destroy, but are behaving like the meanest slave in trying to run away in breach of the contracts and agreements under which you agreed with us the terms of your citizenship. First then answer us this very question - Is it true, what we say, that you have by your own actions made a contract to be a citizen under us, or is it not?' What are we to reply, Crito? Can we do anything but agree?

Crito:- We are bound to agree, Socrates.

Socrates:- 'You agree, then', they would continue, 'that you are breaking contracts and agreements made in person with ourselves, that you did not
E make the agreement under duress, that you were not tricked into it, and that you were not given too little time to make up your mind, but had seventy years in which you were free to depart if we did not please you and you thought our contract unjust. As it is, you did not prefer Sparta or Crete, whose laws (eunomia) you are always praising, or any other city, Greek or barbarian,
33 A but left Athens less often than the lame and the blind and the maimed, so surpassingly did you outdo any other Athenian in your liking for the city and, it follows, for us laws: for who can like a city without liking its laws? After all this, are you now going to fail to stand by the terms of your contract? We at any rate advise you to stick to it, Socrates, and avoid making a mockery of yourself by leaving the city.'

14. TWO DEBATES - MELOS AND SICILY

Melos.

At the end of the year 416, Athens liquidated the Dorian population of the island of Melos. Thucydides gives us a version of the debate that had taken place on Melos in the previous summer between representatives of Athens and the Council of Melos. It is an essay on power-politics, on the imperialists' view that might is right, and also gives an insight into the conflict between democracy and (pro-Spartan) oligarchy.

See Thucydides 5.84-114; 115.4; 116.2-4 (P.358-366) .

Sicily.

At the end of the same year, 416, the Athenians turned to thoughts of conquering Sicily, most of them having no clear idea of the size and population of the island. Nicias and Alcibiades express their conflicting views.

See Thucydides 6.8-9 (P. 371-372); 12-16 (P.375-377); 18.6-end (P.379-380); 24-26 (P. 382-383).

The Lavish Scale of the Sicilian Expedition

In the summer of 415 the whole population of Athens came down to the Piraeus to see the expedition set sail.

See Thucydides 6.31 (P. 385-386).

15. SUSPICION AND CONSPIRACY

The mutilation of the Hermae, and accusations against Alcibiades; the State Galley, Salaminia, is sent to fetch Alcibiades home to stand trial; then Thucydides inserts his account of the murder of Hipparchus and the fate of Harmodius and Aristogeiton (in 514). Cf. the Anonymous Drinking-song, p. 1.

See Thucydides 6.27-29 (P. 383-384); 53 (P.399); 60-61 (P.403-405).

Witch-Hunting

The witch-hunting atmosphere had existed before 415, as can be seen from this extract from the Wasps (422).

Aristophanes, Wasps 482-499

Chorus of Wasps:- At present you don't know what trouble is, but you will know when the counsel for the prosecution pours this same flood of words over you and summons his confederates (synōmotai).

Bdelycleon:- I beg you, by the gods, won't you leave me alone? Or are you
485 determined to tan me and be tanned all day long?

Chorus:- No, I will never leave you, so long as there is anything of me left - you who are set on tyranny over us.

Bdelycleon:- How you do turn everything into 'tyranny' and 'conspirators' (synōmotai), if anyone brings a charge before you, whether it's an important
490 matter or not! I have never heard the word 'tyranny' in the last fifty years, but now it is much cheaper than dried cod; just look how its name is bandied about in the Agora. If a man is buying anchovies and does not want sardines,
495 at once the man who is selling sardines nearby says: "This fellow seems like a man buying luxuries, with a view to tyranny". And if a man asks for leeks as a relish for his sprats, the greengrocer says, with an insolent look: "Tell me, you ask for leeks. Is this with an eye to tyranny? Or do you think Athens should provide your relishes?"

Andocides

ANDOCIDES, born of distinguished parents before the end of the year 440, gained a reputation as a naturally talented speaker, though he regarded the professional rhetorician with disdain. In 415 he found himself hopelessly involved in the accusations following the mutilation of the Hermae. His story is told in the words of his own defence in 399 when he was accused of impiety on the grounds of having taken part in the Mysteries of Eleusis; for he had been debarred from the temples of Attica and from the Athenian Agora as a result of the events of 415. For giving information on the mutilations at that time, he was granted an amnesty (adeia), but this did not prevent the decree of Isotimides, passed later in the same year, from excluding him from Athenian public life. So he went into exile and did not return to Athens until the general amnesty of 403, having appealed in vain for pardon to the Four Hundred and to the restored democracy.

In 415 four informers presented themselves with different instances of profanation; two involved Alcibiades.

Andocides, On the Mysteries 11-18, 34, 36-45, 48-53

11 The Generals (stratēgoi) assigned to Sicily, Nicias, Lamachus, and Alcibiades, had an Assembly called when Lamachus' flagship had already weighed anchor, and Pythonicus rose and spoke among the dēmos: "Men of Athens, you are despatching such a large army and force, and are ready to face danger; but the General Alcibiades I shall prove to you performs secret ceremonies (mystēria) in a house in company with others, and if you vote an amnesty (adeia) to the person for whom I urge it, a servant of one of the men present, though not an initiate, will tell you of the ceremony; should he fail to, deal with me at your
12 discretion, if I do not speak the truth." Alcibiades opposed at length and denied the charge, so the prytaneis decided to remove all the uninitiated, and to go themselves to fetch the lad whom Pythonicus told them to. They went off and fetched a servant of Polemarchus named Andromachus. After they had voted him the necessary amnesty (adeia), he said that secret ceremonies took place in Pulytion's house, and that Alcibiades, Niciades and Melētus were the actual performers, but that others were also present and saw what was going on, and that slaves were present too, as well as himself, his brother, Hicesius the
13 flute-player, and Melētus' slave. He was the first to declare this information,

and he denounced them. Of these Polystratus was arrested and executed, but the others went into exile and you condemned them to death. (To the Clerk of the Court). Please take the records and read their names.

"NAMES . Denounced by Andromachus· Alcibiades, Niciades, Melētus, Archebiades, Archippus, Diogenes, Polystratus, Aristomenes, Oeōnias, Panaetius."

14 This was the first denunciation, gentlemen, made by Andromachus against these men. Now please call Diognētus.
"Were you one of the Commission of Inquiry, Diognētus, when Pythonicus impeached (eisangelia) Alcibiades among the dēmos?" "Yes." "Do you know that Andromachus denounced what went on in Pulytion's house?" "I do". "Are these the names of the men against whom he laid information?" "Yes".

15 Now a second denunciation took place. There was a resident alien (metic) here named Teucer; he had slipped off to Megara but from there offered the Council that, if they granted him an amnesty (adeia), he would lay information about the secret ceremonies, having himself been one of the participants, and against the others who performed them with him, and tell them what he knew about the mutilation of the Hermae. When the Council, possessing plenipotentiary powers (autokratōr), had voted the amnesty, officials went to Megara for him, and he was brought back, having obtained the amnesty (adeia) for himself, and he denounced his companions. These too went into exile because of Teucer's denunciation. Please take the records and read their names.

"NAMES . Denounced by Teucer· Phaedrus, Gniphōnides, Isonomus, Hephaestodōrus, Cēphisodōrus, Diognētus, Smindyrides, Philocrates, Antiphon, Tisarchus, Pantacles, and himself."

Remember, gentlemen, that all this is also being conceded to you.

16 A third denunciation occurred. Alcmeōnides' wife, Agaristē, formerly married to Damōn, gave information that Alcibiades, Axiochus, and Adeimantus performed secret ceremonies in Charmides' house by the Olympieum. All these went into exile as a result of this denunciation.

17 There was still one more denunciation Lydus, the slave of Pherecles from Thēmacus, gave information that secret ceremonies took place in the house of his own master Pherecles at Thēmacus; and among other denunciations he said that my father was present, but was asleep with his face covered. Speusippus, a Councillor, was for handing them over to the jury-court. Then my father appointed sureties and prosecuted Speusippus for making an illegal proposal (graphē paranomōn) and contested the suit before a jury of six thousand Athenians, and won over so many of the jurymen as to leave Speusippus not even two hundred votes. The one who persuaded and urged my father to stay was myself in particular,
18 followed by the rest of his relatives. Please call Callias and Stephanus.

WITNESSES

Call Philippus and Alexippus too. They are relatives of Acumenus and Autocratōr, who went into exile after Lydus' denunciation; Autocratōr is cousin of one, Acumenus uncle of the other. They have reason to detest one who exiled their relatives, and to know particularly whose fault it was that they were exiled. Face the jury, and testify whether I speak the truth . . . .

Andocides goes on to defend his father on this charge and later himself on a charge of informing against his father. He continues:-
34 With regard to the mutilation of the images and the denunciation on the subject, I shall do just as I promised; I shall explain to you from the beginning everything that happened. After Teucer arrived from Megara, having obtained the amnesty (adeia) for himself, he gave the information he possessed about the secret ceremonies and the mutilators of the images, and denounced eighteen men. When these had been denounced, some of them went off into exile, but those who were arrested were executed because of Teucer's denunciation. Please read their names....

36   After this happened, Peisander and Charicles, members of the Commission of
Inquiry and thought at that time to be very well-disposed towards the dēmos,
said that the deeds which had occurred were not the work of a few men but were
designed towards the overthrow of the dēmos, and that investigation must continue
and not cease. The city was in such a state that whenever the Crier proclaimed
that the Council should go to the Council-chamber and he lowered the signal, by
the same signal the Council would go the Council-chamber but those in the Agora

37   would run away, every man afraid of arrest. So, encouraged by the misfortunes
of the city, Diocleides laid an impeachment (eisangelia) before the Council,
declaring he knew the mutilators of the Hermae, and that they numbered about
three hundred, and explained how he had seen them and happened upon the plot.
And I want you, gentlemen, to attend to this and take note of whether I am speaking
the truth, and inform each other; for the speeches were made among you and

38   you are my witnesses to them. He said that he had a slave at Laurium, and
that he had to collect his fee. He had got up early, mistaking the time, and
started walking, under a full moon. When he was by the gateway to Dionysus'
sanctuary, he had seen a lot of men coming down from the Odeion to the dancing-
place (orchēstra), and being afraid of them he had retreated into the shadow and sat
down between the pillar and the monument bearing the bronze statue of the
General. He had seen men numbering about three hundred standing around in
groups of fifteen or twenty; as he saw them facing the moon he recognised the

39   faces of most of them. And first he made up his mind to this, gentlemen, - an
awful thing, in my opinion,-that it was in his power to say that any Athenian he
wished was or was not among these men. After seeing this, he said, he went
to Laurium, and on the next day heard that the Hermae had been muti'ated; so

40   he had realised at once that those men were responsible for the action. On his
return to town he found Commissioners of Inquiry already chosen and reward
for information published as one hundred minae. Seeing Euphēmus the brother
of Callias, Tēlecles' son, sitting in his forge, he took him off to the Hephaesteum
and said just what I have told you, that he had seen us on that night; now, he
said, he did not need to get money from the state for that, so much as from us,
so as to have us as friends. So Euphēmus had said that he had done well to tell
him and had said he should now come to Leōgoras' house "so that you and I may

41   meet Andocides and other essential persons there". He said that he had arrived
on the next day, and actually started knocking at the door, when my father
happened to be coming out and said to him "Is it you the people here are waiting
for? Certainly we mustn't reject such friends." And saying this he went off.
This was how he tried to ruin my father, declaring he was an accomplice.
He said that we said we had decided to give him two talents of silver instead
of the hundred minae offered by the treasury, but that if we obtained what we
wanted, he was to be one of us, and we should exchange pledges to this effect.

42   He had answered that he would think it over, and we told him to come to the
house of Callias, Tēlecles' son, so that he too might be present. Again he was
trying to ruin my relative in this way. He arrived at Callias' house, he said, and
having agreed with us gave a pledge on the Acropolis, and we agreed to pay him
the money in the next month but broke our word and did not pay it. That was
why he had come to denounce what had happened.

43   Such is his impeachment (eisangelia), gentlemen: and he denounces by name
the men whom he said he had recognised, forty-two in all, firstly Mantitheus
and Apsephion, who were Councillors and present at the Council-session, and
then the rest. Peisander rose and said that the decree (psēphisma) passed
in Scamandrius' archonship should be repealed and that those denounced should
be put on the wheel, to make sure that before nightfall they might identify al¹

44   the people. The Council shouted its approval. When Mantitheus and Apsephion
heard this they sat down at the sacred hearth, appealing that they should not be
put on the rack but that they should be granted bail and then tried. They just
succeeded in this, and after appointing the sureties they got on horseback and
went off to the enemy as deserters, leaving the sureties, who had to be exposed

45   to the same treatment as those for whom they were sureties.   At the end of

the session the Council's secret decision to arrest us was carried out, and we were put in the stocks. Then calling up the Generals, they told them to proclaim that those Athenians who lived in the town should take their weapons and go to the Agora. those at the Long Walls to the Thēseum, those at Piraeus to the Agora of Hippodamus, and that even before nightfall a trumpet-call should instruct the cavalry to come to the Anacium; that the Council should go to the Acropolis and sleep there, and the prytaneis in the Tholos. When the Boeotians learnt about the trouble, they had taken the field on the frontier. The man responsible for these misfortunes, Diocleides, they crowned and took on a team of horses to the Town Hall (prytaneion) as saviour of the state, and he had dinner there.

> Andocides, his father and the rest, including a brother of Nicias, were thrown into prison.

48 After we had all been imprisoned in the same place and the prison was closed at nightfall, and we were visited by mother or sister or wife and children, and there was pitiful crying from people in tears and lamentation for our present troubles, Charmides, my cousin, who was of the same age as myself and had

49 been brought up with me from childhood in our house. said to me, "Andocides, you see the extent of our present troubles: in the past I did not need to say anything or to hurt you, but now I am obliged to, because of the disaster which is upon us. For your associates and companions. apart from us your relatives, are either dead or in exile, on the charges for which we are being ruined, having

50 condemned themselves as criminals . . . . If you heard anything of this affair which has happened, speak out, and save first yourself, secondly your father, whom you naturally love dearly, then your brother-in-law, the husband of your only sister, then all your numerous other relations and intimates. and finally me, who throughout my life never hurt you at all, but have been most zealous towards you and your interests, whatever might need to be done."

51 Gentlemen, while Charmides said this, and the rest of them appealed to me , each individual supplicating me, I reflected to myself: "I, above all, have encountered a most dreadful misfortune. Am I to look on while my own relations are unjustly ruined, and are executed and have their property confiscated, and besides have their names inscribed on monuments as sinners against the gods. when they are not responsible for any of what has happened, and further, while three hundred Athenians are exposed to an unjust death penalty, and the city is in the greatest trouble and its people suspicious of each other? Or should I tell the Athenians what I heard from Euphilētus, the very man who did the deed?"

52 Furthermore, on top of this, the following thought came into my head, gentlemen, and I calculated to myself that of those who were offenders and had performed the action some had already been executed after being denounced by Teucer, and others were in exile, with the death-penalty imposed 'in absentia', and only four of the guilty ones had been left undenounced by Teucer, namely Panaetius,

53 Chaeredēmus, Diacritus, and Lysistratus: and it was natural to think that they above all were among those men whom Diocleides had denounced, since they were friends of those already dead. Now for these four safety was not yet secure, while for my kinsmen doom was obvious. unless someone told the Athenians what had happened. Therefore it seemed to me better justly to deprive of their country four men, who are now alive and have returned from exile and enjoy their property, than to let my relations be unjustly executed.

> The Athenians acted upon Andocides' information: Diocleides was put to death and Andocides remained in Athens under the amnesty granted him, until the decree of Isotimides a few months later, see p. 35.

Atimia - disfranchisement

Andocides, On the Mysteries, 73-76

73 For after the fleet was destroyed (in 405) and the siege occurred (in 404), you discussed civic concord, and you decided to enfranchise those who were dis-franchised (atĭmoi) , as proposed by Patrocleides. Who were the disfranchised, and what form did the disfranchisement take for each group? I shall inform you.

Those who owed money to the treasury, all those who had lost on audit (euthūnai)
after holding office, or were guilty of failing to carry out court orders , or lost
public lawsuits or had summary fines imposed on them, or after buying tax-
collecting privileges had failed to pay the sum agreed, or after acting as sureties
for the treasury had failed to pay: all these had to make payment during the
ninth prytany, otherwise their debts were doubled and their possessions sold.

74 This was one form of disfranchisement (atīmia), but another consisted of those
whose persons were disfranchised, but who retained and enjoyed possession of their property, in this second group were all those who were convicted of embezzlement
or bribery. These and their descendants were to be disfranchised. All
those who deserted their posts or were convicted of avoiding military service
or cowardice in the field or avoiding a naval battle or throwing away their shields,
or were convicted three times of giving false testimony or three times of falsely
claiming to have witnessed a summons, or who misused their parents - all these

75 had their persons disfranchised, but kept their property. Others again were
disfranchised "according to specifications", not totally, but partially; for example,
soldiers who, because they had stayed in the city at the time of the Four Hundred,
in other respects had the same rights as the other citizens, but were not permitted
to speak in the Assembly of the dēmos or be Councillors . Those were the
privileges from which this group was disfranchised, for that was the specification
for them. Others did not have the right to prosecute publicly, others to lay
information before an official. For others the specification was not to sail to
the Hellespont, for others not to Ionia, for others not to enter the Agora.

A Watch-dog of the People

Part of a speech by Athenagoras, prostatēs tou dēmou, at Syracuse, in 415.
Syracuse, as Thucydides says, was a city of similar size and institutions to Athens,
and the views on politics here expressed may be taken as thoroughly Athenian,
and representing the feelings of, say, Alcibiades' opponents in the Assembly.

See Thucydides 6. 38-39. 2 (P. 391-392).

16. TREACHERY OF ALCIBIADES - DECELEIA

Parts of a cynical and traitorous speech put by Thucydides into the
mouth of Alcibiades after he had escaped from Sicily to Sparta.

See Thucydides 6. 89 (P.422-423); 91.5 - 9 . 4 (P. 424-425).

Results of the Occupation of Deceleia.

In this passage, dealing with the economic and financial straits of Athens
in 413, Thucydides (as usual in economic matters) does not give as much
detail as we should like.

See Thucydides 7. 27-28 (P. 447-449).

17. REVOLUTION

The first reaction in Athens to news of the Sicilian disaster; the
machinations of Alcibiades; Thucydides' account of the revolution
of the Four Hundred, which is supplemented and partly contradicted
by Aristotle, Constitution of Athens 29ff, p. 40 .; the death of
Hyperbolus is mentioned in passing; Alcibiades in Samos after the
establishment of a democratic regime in exile there; discontent
with the Four Hundred; the defeat of an Athenian fleet off Euboea.

See Thucydides 8.1 (P.489-490); 47-49 (P.514-516) and 53-54 (P. 518-519);
63.3-64.1 (P. 523) and 65-70 (P. 524-528) and 72 (P. 528-529); 73.3 (P.529);
86 (P. 537-538); 89.3-4 (P. 540); 97 (P. 547).

The Effects of Stasis

Thucydides' general comments on stasis in war-time are given in the context of the revolution at Corcyra in 426: but his remarks clearly apply in large measure to Athens at the time of the Four Hundred. For the general tone of the passage, cf. Thucydides 2.53 (P. 126-127) and Plato, Seventh Letter, p. 53.

See Thucydides 3.82.2-83 (P.208-211).

'Aristotle' on the Revolution

The reader will note the discrepancies between this account of the Four Hundred and that of Thucydides 63.3 - 64.1 (P.523) and 65-70 (P.524-528).

Aristotle, Constitution of Athens 29, 31-33

29.1 So long as the two sides were equally balanced during the war, they retained the democracy. But after the disaster in Sicily, the Spartan side gained superiority through their alliance with the King of Persia; at this point the Athenians had to overthrow their democracy and set up the constitution of the Four Hundred. The speech in favour of this resolution (psēphisma) was made by Melobius, and the resolution itself had been drafted by Pythodōrus from Anaphlystos: but the main reason was the acquiescence of the multitude (hoi polloi) in their belief that the Great King would give them more aid in the

2 war if they set up an oligarchic constitution. The resolution (psēphisma) of Pythodōrus read as follows: 'In addition to the ten probouloi already in existence, the dēmos should elect twenty more from those over forty years of age: these should take an oath to make whatever proposals they considered to be in the best interests of the state, and should then make proposals for the public security: any other person who wanted to, should be free to propose a measure, to allow

3 them to choose the one that was best of all'. Cleitophon moved an amendment to the resolution of Pythodōrus, that the probouloi who were elected should conduct an investigation into the ancestral laws passed by Cleisthenes in founding the democracy, so that with these in mind they could advise the best possible course, on the grounds that Cleisthenes' constitution was not democratic but was similar to Solon's. When elected the probouloi first moved that it

4 should be compulsory for the prytaneis to put to the vote all proposals made for the public security, and they then repealed the procedures for illegal proposals (graphai paranomōn), for impeachments (eisangeliai), and for summonses, so that any Athenians who wanted to, might give advice about the matters under discussion. They then moved that anyone who attempted to penalise or prosecute or bring them to trial for what they were doing, should be liable to be denounced and brought before the Generals (stratēgoi), who were to hand them over to

5 the Eleven for execution. They subsequently drew up the constitution as follows: 'It should be illegal to spend public funds on anything but war; all officials should carry out their duties unpaid for the duration of the war, except for the nine archons and the prytaneis who were to receive three obols each per day; all the rest of the government (politeia) should be entrusted for the duration of the war to those Athenians who in person and property were most capable (dunatoi) of perform- ing state services (leitourgein), to be not less than five thousand in number; they were to be empowered to make treaties with anyone they wished; and they were to elect from each tribe ten men over forty years of age to enrol the Five Thousand, after taking an oath over unblemished victims'.

Chapter 30 deals with a constitutional plan that was never adopted.

31.1 This then was the constitution that they drew up for the future, but for the existing crisis it was to be as follows: There was to be a Council of Four Hundred, according to ancestral custom, forty from each tribe from a preliminary list elected by their fellow-tribesmen from those over the age of thirty; these were to appoint the officials, draft a proposal about the form of the oath to be taken, and take whatever action they considered suitable concerning the laws and the

2   officials' accounts (euthūnai) and any other matters; they were to keep to
whatever laws were enacted concerning the government of the state, and were
not empowered to alter them or enact others; for the time being the Generals
were to be elected from all the Five Thousand, but as soon as the Council was
appointed, it was to hold a review under arms and select ten men for the job,
and a secretary (grammateus) for them; those selected were to hold office
with plenipotentiary powers (autokratores) for the following year, and to hold

3   consultations with the Council on any matter they wanted to. They were to select
also one cavalry commander (hipparchos) and ten commanders of each tribe's
cavalry division (phylarchoi); for the future the Council was to conduct the
election of these officials according to the regulations laid down; of the other
officials none but the Council and the Generals should be permitted to hold the
same office more than once; for the future, in order that the Four Hundred
might be divided into four lists, when the ordinary citizens took their turn
to form the Council with the others, the hundred men were to divide them into
sections.

32.1   This then was the constitution drawn up by the Hundred, who were elected
by the Five Thousand. These proposals were put to the vote by Aristomachus
and carried by the plēthos. The Council for Kallias' archonship (412/411) was
dissolved on the 14th day of the month of Thargēlion (May/June) before completing
its term of office. The Four Hundred took up office on the 21st of Thargēlion,
whereas the normal Council elected by lot would have taken up office on the 14th

2   of Skirophorion (June/July). This was how the oligarchy was established in the
archonship of Kallias, about a hundred years after the expulsion of the tyrants.
Those chiefly responsible were Peisander, Antiphon and Thēramenes, men of

3   good birth and highly thought of for their insight and judgement. After the establishment of this constitution, the selection of the Five Thousand was purely nominal,
while it was the Four Hundred, together with the ten Generals with plenipotentiary
powers (autokratores), who entered the Council-chamber and governed the state.
They made overtures to Sparta for an end to hostilities on the basis of the status
quo. But the Spartans would not consider it unless Athens also relinquished her

33.1   command of the sea, so in the end they abandoned the idea. The constitution of
the Four Hundred lasted for perhaps four months, for two of which Mnēsilochus
was archon, in the year of the archonship of Theopompus (411/410), who
received the office for the remaining ten months. But when they were defeated
in the sea-battle off Eretria, and the whole of Euboea except Oreos revolted, they
were upset by this disaster more than by any that had yet occurred; for they were
sustained more by Euboea than by Attica. So they dissolved the Four Hundred
and handed over power to the Five Thousand who were capable of equipping

2   themselves as hoplites, after voting that no public office should be paid. Those
chiefly responsible for the overthrow of the Four Hundred were Aristocrates
and Thēramenes, who disapproved of their proceedings. For they took all
decisions themselves, and referred nothing to the Five Thousand. Athens
appears to have been well governed during this critical period, when in a time of
war, political rights (politeia) were confined to those of hoplite status.

Antiphon

ANTIPHON was born c.480 of an aristocratic family. He became the
first of the 'logographoi' (professional speech-writers), and his success
in defending supporters of oligarchy later gained him influence in the
oligarchic hetaireiai. The following is a fragment of a speech Antiphon
himself delivered in his defence 'On the Charge of Treason' in 411. Only
three other much smaller fragments of this important speech survive.
It is thought that the speech itself may have served the writer of 'Aristotle',
Constitution of Athens 29-32 as his main source for the events of 411.

Antiphon, On a Charge of Treason, Fragment

(Did I desire a revolution) because after being elected to public office I had
handled large funds and had to face an audit (euthūnai) which I feared? Or

because I was disfranchised (atīmos)? Because I had done you some injury? Or because I feared an impending lawsuit? Not at all, because none of these applied to me. Then was it because you had taken my property away from me?
5   Or because you had punished me for some wrong committed by my ancestors? For these are motives inducing some to desire a different form of government (politeia) from the established one, in order that they may either avoid being punished for crimes or obtain vengeance for wrongs suffered and prevent their
10 repetition. But nothing of this sort applied to me. The prosecutors assert, however, that I assisted others in writing speeches for use in court, and that the Four Hundred profited from this. Now under the oligarchy this would not have been possible for me, but under the democracy I am the gainer; from the art of oratory I was unlikely to be of any significance under the oligarchy, while
15 under the democracy I would be important, wouldn't I? Well now, how is it likely that I should desire an oligarchy? Am I incapable of reasoning this out for myself, or am I the only Athenian who does not recognise what his own advantages are?

The following passages are taken from Pseudo-Plutarch's Life of Antiphon, 23-24, and are thought to be genuine quotations from a collection of Athenian historical inscriptions made by a certain Craterus in the third century B.C. The first is the official indictment of Antiphon and two collaborators.

Pseudo-Plutarch, Life of Antiphon, 23-24

23 Resolved by the Council on the twenty-first day of the prytany : secretary (grammateus) Dēmonicus from Alōpekē: president (epistatēs) Philostratus from Pallēnē: proposed by Andron:- With regard to the men whom the Generals declare went as ambassadors to Sparta to the detriment of the city of Athens, both taking ship from the camp on an enemy vessel and returning overland through Deceleia Archeptolemus, Onomacles and Antiphon are to be arrested and delivered to the jury-court to be punished. And the Generals and such of the Council as the Generals think fit to choose to aid them, up to a total of ten, are to present them in court in order that they may stand trial in person. And the thesmothetae are to summon them to-morrow, and when the summonses have expired, they are to bring them to the jury-court on a charge of treason. And the selected prosecutors and the Generals and anyone else who wishes, are to accuse them. And any of them whom the jury-court finds guilty shall be dealt with in accordance with the existing law about traitors.

The second passage is the text of their conviction, though it will be noted that Onomacles' name is omitted.

24 Found guilty of treason: Archeptolemus, son of Hippodamus, from Agrylē, being present; Antiphon, son of Sōphilus, from Rhamnūs, being present. The penalty was assessed that these two were to be handed over to the Eleven and their property be confiscated and a tithe given to the Goddess: their houses to be razed to the ground and memorial-stones erected on the foundations, with the inscription:- "Here lived Archeptolemus and Antiphon, the traitors": and the two mayors (demarchs) were to publish an inventory of their property; and it was to be illegal to bury Archeptolemus and Antiphon at Athens or in the Athenian empire, and Archeptolemus and Antiphon were to be disfranchised (atīmos), and their descendants too, both legitimate and illegitimate, and if anyone adopts any of the descendants of Archeptolemus or Antiphon, the adopter is to be disfranchised (atīmos). This is to be inscribed on a pillar of bronze, and erected in the same place as the decrees (psēphismata) concerning Phrynichus.

Polystratus

This speech was spoken by the son of Polystratus in defence of his father on trial in 410 for offences against the democracy. Polystratus, though seemingly of moderate views, was a member of the Four Hundred. He was fined heavily in 411 by Thēramenes' government, though he had been a

registrar of the Five Thousand and was brought to trial again in 410 by
the restored democracy.

Mistakenly ascribed to Lysias, this speech is an example of the amateurish
efforts at law that gave rise to the professional speech-writers (logographoi)
of whom Lysias was one.

(Lysias) 20.1-3, 11-16

1   I do not think you should grow angry at the name of the Four Hundred, but at the
actions of some of their members. For while there were some who had plotted
against the state, the rest had no intention of doing any harm either to the state
or to any of you, but joined the Council with good intentions: the defendant,

2   Polystratus, is one of this group. He was selected by his fellow-tribesmen for
being a respectable man (chrēstos) both in his dealings with his fellow-demesmen and
with you, the plēthos ; yet he is prosecuted for ill-will towards you, the plēthos,
after he has been selected by his fellow-tribesmen, who could best determine

3   the qualities of their own members. Then to what purpose would he have desired
an oligarchy?   Because he was young enough to make a hit among you as an orator,
or because he relied upon his physique to enable him to do violence (hubris) to any
of your number?   But you can see how old he is, of an age which actually qualifies
him to discourage others from such behaviour. ....

11   Yet in their previous prosecution (in 411) they made false accusations against my
father, especially saying that Phrynichus was a relative of his. Now if anyone
wishes, let him bear witness, during my own speaking-time, that he was related
to Phrynichus. In fact their accusation was false. Indeed he was not even a

12   friend of his by upbringing. Phrynichus was a poor, country shepherd, while my
father was being educated in Athens. On growing up he started farming, but
Phrynichus came to town and became a professional informer (sycophant); you
can see that they had no qualities in common. Moreover, when Phrynichus was
due to pay a fine to the treasury, my father did not contribute his portion to him,
though it is in such situations that it is most obvious who a man's friends are. If
he was a fellow-demesman, that is no justification for my father's suffering harm,

13   unless you too are guilty because he is a fellow-citizen of yours. How could
anyone be a greater friend of the dēmos than a man who, after you had voted for
assigning the government to the Five Thousand, as registrar made a list of nine
thousand, so that none of his fellow-demesmen might be at odds with him, but
so that he might enrol any who wished to join, and so do a favour should anyone

14   not be qualified (as a hoplite).   Well, it is not those who augment the citizen-
body who overthrow democracy, but those who diminish it. He was unwilling
either to take the oath or to act as registrar, but they forced him to do so,
imposing fines and penalties; and when he was forced and had taken the oath, he
attended the Council for only eight days and then went on the naval expedition to
Eretria, and there in the naval battles he had the reputation of being no coward (not ponēros),
and he returned home wounded, when the revolution was just over. The defendant,
who had neither proposed any motion nor attended the Council for more than eight
days, incurred that large fine, while of those who opposed you in their speeches

15   and were continually in the Council, many have been acquitted. I speak not in envy
of them, but in pity for my father and myself; for some who were thought guilty
have been begged off by those who in government showed their enthusiasm for
your interests, but others, who were guilty, bought off their accusers and were

16   not even thought guilty. Surely then our condition, if condemned would be deplorable?
They accuse the Four Hundred of crime, yet you yourselves were persuaded by them
to hand over the government to the Five Thousand, and if you, with all your numbers,
were persuaded, ought not each one of the Four Hundred to have been persuaded too?
But it is not these who are guilty, but those who deceived and injured you. The
defendant among many facts points out to you that if he really desired any
revolutionary activity (neōterizein) against you, the plēthos, he would never
have gone off to sea within eight days of joining the Council.

18.   THE YEARS OF DECLINE

Some Views of Socrates on the Decline of Athens

> This conversation, put into the mouths of Socrates and the younger Pericles (son of Pericles and Aspasia), is to be imagined taking place c.410.   The views of Socrates are overlaid with the views of XENOPHON - soldier, country-squire and admirer of Sparta - writing c.360.

Xenophon, Memorabilia 3.5. 13-22

13   "Yes, Socrates", said Pericles, "and I am surprised how far downhill our city has gone."
"My belief," replied Socrates, "is that, just as some athletes are in a class of their own and easily carry off the prizes but through slackness then fall behind their rivals, so the Athenians used to enjoy a great superiority but have since become careless of themselves and consequently have declined."

14   "How, then, can they now recover their old excellence (aretē)?" asked Pericles.

"I don't think that is at all mysterious.   If they find out the customs of their ancestors and practice them as well as they did, they will become as good as they were;   or failing that, if they at least imitate those who are now pre-eminent and practice their customs, they will be as good as them if they follow their customs equally carefully, - or even better, if they are more careful."

15   "I take it you're saying that the city has a long way to go before it can claim to be a city of true gentlemen (kalok'agathia).   For when will the Athenians show respect for older men, as the Spartans do, instead of despising their elders, beginning with their own fathers?   When will they adopt the Spartan method of training, instead of neglecting their own physical fitness and even laughing

16   at those who pay regard to it?   When will they be as obedient to those in official positions as the Spartans are, instead of taking a pride in despising them?   When will the Athenians reach the Spartan degree of civic concord?   For instead of co-operating with one another for the general good, the Athenians prefer to direct their abuse and envy at themselves rather than against the rest of mankind; they are the most quarrelsome of men at both private and public meetings;   they most often bring lawsuits against one another;   they prefer to derive profit in that sort of way at each other's expense rather than by mutual assistance; and although they view public affairs as alien to themselves, they nonetheless fight over them and find their greatest joy in their capacity for such matters.

17   As a result, mischief and evil are rife in the city, and enmity and mutual hatred breed abundantly among our citizens;   that's why I am always terrified that some evil beyond our power to endure may befall the city."

18   "No, Pericles," replied Socrates, "don't think that the Athenians are suffering from such an incurable malaise (ponēria).   Don't you see how disciplined they are in the fleets, how well-behaved they are in obeying the umpires at athletic contests, and how they are second to none in assisting their chorus-instructors?"

19   "It certainly is remarkable," said Pericles, "that men like these show obedience towards their masters, whereas the infantry (hoplītes) and cavalry, who are supposed to be the pick of the citizens for true gentlemanliness (kalok'agathia), are the least disciplined of all."

20   Socrates then asked:- "Is not the Court of the Areopagus composed, Pericles, of men who have proved their worth?"
"Yes, certainly," he answered.
"Do you know then of any men who judge lawsuits and perform all their other functions more excellently or more fairly or with greater dignity or justice?"
"I make no criticism of these men."
"So you ought not to despair of Athenian discipline."

21   "But still, in the forces, where there is the greatest need for restraint (sōphrosynē), discipline and obedience, they ignore all these qualities," said Pericles.

"In that case, perhaps they are under the command of incompetent officers. Surely you have seen that no one tries to give orders to lyre-players or to members of the chorus or to dancers, if he is incompetent, nor to wrestlers or to those who box as well as wrestle (pankratiastai)? All who give such orders are able to show their subordinates where they obtained this knowledge;
22   but most of our <u>Generals</u> just improvise. However, I don't suppose you come into that category."

The Return of Alcibiades

Alcibiades, while still in exile, was elected General in 408. Thereupon he cautiously approached his native city.

Xenophon, Hellenica 1.4. 12-21

12   When he realised that the Athenians were well disposed towards him and that his supporters had elected him <u>General</u> and were privately urging his return, he sailed back, arriving at the Piraeus on the day of the festival of the <u>Plyntēria</u> when the statue of the goddess Athena had been veiled, a coincidence that some pronounced inauspicious, both for himself and for the city; for on this day no
13   Athenian would venture to set his hand to any important business. As he sailed in, the rabble (<u>ochlos</u>) from the Piraeus and from the city thronged in wonder to the dockside, longing to see the famous Alcibiades.
Some said he was the greatest Athenian and had been the only one to be unjustly exiled. Plots had been laid against him by those less influential (<u>dunamenoi</u>) than himself whose accusations were more wicked (<u>mochthēra</u>) and whose policies were self-seeking. Alcibiades however had augmented the community's wealth
14   out of his own resources and those of the state, and had been prepared to stand trial on the spot when charged with profanation of the mysteries, but his adversaries had postponed what seemed to be a just request and in his absence
15   deprived him of his citizenship. In this period he was forced by stress of circumstances to be a slave and to pay court to Athens' bitterest enemies, daily running the risk of losing his life. Though he could see his own citizens and kinsmen, indeed the whole city, erring grievously, he was prevented by exile
16   from helping them. They urged that it was uncharacteristic of men like Alcibiades to want change or revolution. For he had the advantage, under the democracy, of a position higher than any of his equals in age and not inferior to his elders; while it was the fortune of his enemies, though they had the same reputation as before, when they subsequently rose to power, to put out of the way the best men (<u>beltistoi</u>) in Athens, and then, because there were no other best men (beltistoi) left, to be tolerated by the citizens for the simple reason that they could
17   not find anyone better. Others said that he alone was responsible for the trouble that had been theirs in the past, and that he alone perhaps was the prime mover of the perils that now threatened the city.
18   When his ship reached its anchorage, Alcibiades did not immediately disembark for fear of his enemies, but stood on deck looking to see if his friends were there.
19   When he caught sight of his cousin, Euryptolemus, the son of Peisianax, and his other relatives and friends with them, he disembarked and went up to the city
20   accompanied by men ready to prevent any attack on his person. In the Council and the Assembly he maintained that he had not profaned the mysteries but had been unjustly treated. Other such statements were made without any opposition, for the Assembly would not have stood for it, and he was elected General with plenipotentiary powers (<u>autokratōr</u>), in the belief that he was capable of restoring Athens to her former power. The war had obliged the Athenians to conduct the procession of the mysteries (to Eleusis) by sea, but, as his first act, Alcibiades
21   marched the whole army out in force to escort the procession by land. Afterwards he reviewed the army, one thousand five hundred infantry (<u>hoplītes</u>) , one hundred and fifty cavalry and a hundred ships.

After about four months in Athens, Alcibiades left for Samos.   The
Assembly soon lost confidence in him again, and after a fatal mistake
by one of his subordinates he was removed from his command.   He
withdrew to the Chersonnese and never returned again to Athens.

Democracy in Decline

Aristotle, Constitution of Athens 34, 1-2

1   But these men (the Four Hundred, or, according to others, the Five Thousand)
were soon deprived of their political power (politeia) by the dēmos.   In the
sixth year after the overthrow of the Four Hundred, in the archonship of Kallias
from Angelē (406/405), after the sea-battle at Arginusae, it came about first
that the ten Generals responsible for the naval victory were all condemned by
a single vote, though some of them had not even taken part in the battle, while
others had been picked up from the sea by someone else's vessel;   for the dēmos
were completely deceived by agitators who roused their anger.   Next, the Spartans
offered to evacuate Decelea and make peace on the basis of the status quo.   Some
were eager to accept this, but the majority (plēthos) rejected it, for they were
deceived by Cleophon, who prevented the conclusion of peace by coming into the
Assembly drunk and wearing a breastplate, and protesting that he would not allow
it unless the Spartans handed over all the cities (previously subject to Athens).

2   This was a serious error, but it did not take long before they realised their
mistake.   For in the next year, in the archonship of Alexias (405/404), they
met with disaster in the naval battle at Aegospotami, as a result of which the
city fell into the hands of Lysander, who established the rule of the Thirty.

Trial of the Generals (stratēgoi) after Arginusae

The Generals defeated the enemy at Arginusae in 406, but failed to rescue
all their own sailors from the water because of bad weather.   The subsequent trial provides an example of eisangelia;   it is also a conspicuous
example of the ingratitude of the dēmos to its Generals.

Xenophon, Hellenica 1.7. 1-29. 33-35

1   The Athenians at home suspended these Generals (stratēgoi), with the exception
of Conon, and elected Adeimantus and Philodes as his colleagues.   Two of the
Generals who had fought at Arginusae. Protomachus and Aristogenes, did not

2   return to Athens; but when the other six, Pericles, Diomedon, Lysias, Aristocrates,
Thrasyllus and Erasinides, arrived. Archedēmus, who at that time was prostatēs
tou dēmou in Athens and in charge of the diōbelia. imposed a fine upon Erasinides
and brought a criminal charge against him in the jury-court, accusing him of
being in possession of public funds from the Hellespont and also making charges
about his conduct as General.   The jury-court decided to have him imprisoned.

3   After this the Generals gave the Council a report of the sea-battle and the
violence of the storm.   On the proposal of Timocrates that the rest of them
should also be imprisoned and handed over to the dēmos in the Assembly, the

4   Council ordered their arrest.   After that a meeting of the Assembly was held
at which a number of men led by Thēramenes brought charges against the
Generals, saying they ought to offer a justification for their failure to pick up
the ship-wrecked crews;   as proof that the Generals were not blaming anyone
else, Thēramenes produced a despatch which the Generals had sent to the
Council and to the Assembly in which they attributed their failure entirely to

5   the storm.   After this each of the Generals in a brief defence,- for they were
not (yet) being given a proper legal hearing,- related what had happened;   before
they themselves sailed against the enemy, they had given orders to Thēramenes,
Thrasybulus and other equally competent trierarchs, who had previously served

6   as Generals, to pick up the ship-wrecked crews;   so that if anybody was to be
blamed in connection with the rescue operations it could be nobody but those who
had received these orders.   "Not that we intend, " they said, "to repeat the
falsehood in the accusation made against us by saying that our accusers were
themselves to blame;   it was only the violence of the storm that prevented the

7   rescue". To support their account they offered to produce as witnesses the helmsmen and many others of the crews. These statements appeared convincing to the Assembly, and many private citizens stood up and offered to go bail for the Generals; but as by this time it was too late for a show of hands to be seen, it was decided to adjourn the Assembly and let the Council draw up a preliminary resolution (probouleuma) about the form their trial should take.

8   After this the festival of the Apaturia began, which was an occasion for fathers of families and their relatives to meet. At the festival supporters of Theramenes procured a large number of men to come to the Assembly, wearing black and with their heads shaved, as if they were relatives of the dead,

9   and put pressure on Callixenus to accuse the Generals in the Council. When the Assembly met, the Council reported its motion proposed by Callixenus in the following words:

"Whereas at the last Assembly a hearing has been given to the Generals' accusers and to the Generals in their own defence, all Athenians shall record their votes. tribe by tribe. Two urns shall be set up for the use of each tribe, and for each tribe a crier shall make proclamation that any man who finds the Generals guilty of failing to rescue the victorious sailors shall cast his vote in the first urn, and

10   any who finds them not guilty in the second urn. If they are found guilty they shall incur the penalty of death and be handed over to the Eleven; their property shall be confiscated and one tenth part given to the goddess (Athena)."

11   One man came up to the platform and said he had been saved by clinging on to a barley-barrel, and that the drowning men had charged him, if he survived, to tell the demos that the Generals had failed to pick up their country's heroes.

12   Euryptolemus, son of Peisianax, and others wanted to summons Callixenus for illegal procedure (graphe paranomon); but though some of the demos supported them, the majority (plethos) protested that it was scandalous that

13   anybody should prevent the demos from doing what it wanted to do. At that Lyciscus proposed that, if they did not drop the summons, they too should be put on trial by the same vote as the Generals; and when the rabble (ochlos) again

14   cheered at this, they were forced to drop it. Some of the prytaneis said they would refuse to put such an illegal proposal to the vote, but Callixenus again came forward and proposed to include the prytaneis too in the accusation, while

15   others shouted for the summoning of those who refused. So all the prytaneis except Socrates, son of Sophroniscus, who said he would not break the law, were frightened into agreeing to put it to the vote.

16   Then Euryptolemus came up to the platform and made a speech on behalf of the Generals:

"Men of Athens," he said, "I rise partly to accuse and partly to defend my friends Pericles, who is a relation of mine, and Diomedon, and at the same time to give

17   the best advice I can for the city as a whole. My accusation is that they dissuaded their colleagues from sending a despatch to the Council and to your Assembly, reporting that they had given orders to Theramenes and Thrasybulus to take 47 triremes and pick up the ship-wrecked crews and that those officers failed

18   to do so. In consequence are they now to share the blame for what Theramenes and Thrasybulus, on their own responsibility, failed to do? And in return for the humanity which they showed to these men at that time, are they now to risk losing their lives because of the intrigues of these men and certain others?

19   But they will not succeed if you listen to me, if you obey the law and your consciences, and so give.yourselves the best chance to ascertain the truth and to avoid the remorse you will feel when you find too late that you have committed the supreme sin against Heaven and against yourselves. This is my advice; it leaves no room for you to be misled by me or by anybody else; you will know who are guilty and punish them, together or individually, by any form of trial you choose, without relying on anybody's judgment except your own. But just give them one day - more if you like - to make their own defence.

20   You all know the decree (psephisma) of Cannonus, gentlemen, and its extreme severity. Under that decree if a man commits a crime against the demos

of Athens he is to make his defence standing in chains before the dēmos; if found
guilty he shall die by being thrown into the pit, his property shall be confiscated
21 and one tenth given to the goddess. I propose that the Generals should be tried
under that decree - yes indeed, if you like, you can start with Pericles, my own
relative; I should be ashamed to value him more highly than the city of Athens
22 as a whole. Or, if you prefer, try them under the law which applies to temple-
robbers and traitors, that any man who attempts to betray the city or to steal
sacred property shall be tried in a jury-court and if found guilty shall be refused
23 burial in Attica and his property shall be given to the state. Choose whichever
of these laws you like, gentlemen, but let each man have a separate trial.
Divide the day into three parts, one third for you to assemble and (later) to give
24 your verdicts, one third for the prosecution, and one third for the defence. If this
is done, the guilty will be punished with the utmost severity, those who are
not responsible will be set free by your hands, gentlemen, instead of being made
25 innocent victims, and you yourselves will keep your honour and your oath by
conducting the trial in accordance with the law instead of collaborating with the
Spartans by illegally executing without a trial the victors who robbed Sparta of
26 70 of her ships. Why are you in such a desperate hurry? What are you
afraid of? Are you afraid that a legal trial, instead of the illegal single vote
that Callixenus persuaded the Council to recommend to the dēmos, will prevent
27 you from putting to death or releasing anyone you like? But remember; you
might put to death an innocent man and be sorry later on. Remorse is tragic:
by that time it is too late to do any good, especially when your mistake has
28 cost a man his life. When Aristarchus not long ago (in 411) overthrew the
democracy and went on to betray Oenoē to our enemies the Thebans, you gave
him a day to make his defence as he pleased and allowed him all his other
legal rights. It would be a monstrous thing if you did not grant the same
29 rights to the Generals, these conquerors who have never failed you? No, men
of Athens! The laws of Athens are your laws. It is to them you owe your
greatness. Try to preserve them and do not attempt to do anything without
their sanction."

He goes on to recount the facts of the case, and concludes:

33 "So, men of Athens, do not respond to victory and success as if it were defeat
and failure! Do not show ingratitude when confronted by the irresistible act
of God by giving a verdict of treachery instead of helplessness, because they
were powerless to carry out their orders in the face of the storm! Justice
demands instead that you should wreathe the victors' brows with laurels and
turn a deaf ear to the worthless (ponēroi) men who would condemn them to
death!"

34 With these words Euryptolemus proposed a motion that the men should be tried
individually under the decree (psēphisma) of Cannōnus: the Council's motion
was that they should all be tried together on a single vote. A show of hands
was taken to decide between the two motions, and at first that of Euryptolemus
was carried; but when Menecles lodged an objection under oath, a second vote
was taken and the Council's motion was carried. After that the eight Generals
who had fought the battle were found guilty and the six present were put to death.
35 But it was not long before the Athenians regretted their action and passed a
decree (psēphisma) that complaints should be lodged against those who had misled
the dēmos, specifically including Callixenus, and that these men should give
sureties until their trial. Complaints were lodged against four others besides
Callixenus and they were kept under arrest by their guarantors; but later,
during the stasis in the course of which Cleophon was put to death, they escaped
before being brought to trial. Afterwards when the men from the Piraeus
returned to Athens (in 403), Callixenus came back but died of starvation, an
object of universal hatred.

Lysias on Thēramenes

LYSIAS (c.458-379), born of Syracusan parents who settled as metics
in the Piraeus, spent his early manhood in Thurii studying rhetoric
under the Sicilian Tisias. He returned to Athens in 412 and with his
elder brother, Polemarchus, became interested in the new intellectual
movement of the Socratic circle. For support of the democratic cause
in its difficult years he would have been awarded Athenian citizenship in
403 but for a technical mistake in procedure; instead he spent the rest
of his life writing speeches for other men to deliver. We know most
about his gifts from Plato's Phaedrus and from his own speech against the
oligarch Eratosthenes for the murder of Polemarchus, from which the
following extract on Thēramenes is taken. Lysias himself delivered this
speech, probably in 403/402.

Lysias 12. 62-70

62 Listen now, and I will instruct you about Thēramenes too, as briefly as I can.
I urge you to listen for the sake of the city and myself, and let it not cross anyone's
mind that when Eratosthenes is on trial I am accusing Thēramenes. I am
informed that Eratosthenes intends to use as defence his friendship and partner-
63 ship with Thēramenes. I suppose, indeed, that if his political career had been
associated with Themistocles he would have been eager to claim that he acted to
secure the construction of the walls, when he claims that he worked with
Thēramenes for their demolition. In fact I do not think they deserve equal
acclaim, for Themistocles built the walls against the desire of the Spartans,
64 but Thēramenes demolished them after cheating his fellow-citizens. Thus
the city has experienced the opposite of what was expected. For it was proper
for Thēramenes' friends to share his downfall, except for any who happened
to oppose him: but now I see that his name is quoted in court by defendants as
justification, and that his associates try to gain credit, as if he had been respon-
65 sible, not for great disasters, but for many benefits. To start with, he was
primarily responsible for the earlier oligarchy, having persuaded you to choose
the government (politeia) of the Four Hundred. His father was one of the probouloi
and did the same, but he himself, reputed to be very well-disposed to the govern-
66 ment was elected a General by them. As long as he enjoyed privileges he
showed himself loyal to the city; but after he saw that Peisander, Callaeschrus,
and others were gaining precedence over him, while you, the plēthos, were no
longer willing to listen to them, then both through jealousy of them and in fear
67 of you he co-operated with Aristocrates. Desiring to be thought loyal to you,
the plēthos, he prosecuted Antiphon and Archeptolemus, his close friends, and
procured their execution, and reached such depths of villainy that he simultaneously
enslaved you to gain credit with them and destroyed his friends to gain credit
with you
68 Privileged and highly esteemed, he himself proclaimed his intention to save the
city and yet he himself destroyed it, declaring he had made a great and valuable
discovery. He promised to bring about a peace without giving hostages or
demolishing the walls or surrendering the fleet; he refused to tell anyone its
69 character, but urged men to trust him. Though the Council of the Areopagus
was taking measures for security, and many spoke against Thēramenes,
and though you knew that others were observing secrecy on account of the enemy,
while he had refused to mention among his own fellow-citizens what he was
going to tell the enemy, you, men of Athens, nevertheless entrusted him with
70 your country, your children, your wives, your very selves. None of his
promises did he fulfil, but he was so determined that the city must become
small and weak that he persuaded you to do things which none of the enemy
had ever mentioned or any of the citizens ever anticipated, - not under con-
straint from the Spartans, but through the proposals he himself made to them,
namely the demolition of the walls of the Piraeus and the abolition of the
existing constitution - knowing full well that if you were not deprived of all
hope for the future, you would exact swift retribution from him.

Thēramenes' Defence of his Policies

Thēramenes took a leading part in the eventual peace negotiations in 404
after Aegospotami and became one of 'the Thirty', the body appointed
under Spartan pressure to rule Athens. But he found the Thirty (as
previously he had found the Four Hundred) too arbitrary and tyrannical
for his liking. His colleague Critias accused him before the Council
of double-dealing, but after Thēramenes' speech in defence of his policies,
the end of which is given here, the Council were ready to acquit him;
so Critias and the armed supporters of the Thirty took the law into their
own hands and forced him to drink hemlock.

Xenophon, Hellenica 2. 3. 47-49

47   "Critias calls me 'the stage boot' (kothornos), because, as he says, I try to fit
both parties. But what in the name of heaven should we call the man who
pleases neither party? For in the democracy you, Critias, were regarded
as the bitterest enemy of the dēmos (mīsodēmotatos), and under the aristocracy
you have become the bitterest enemy of the respectable (chrēstoi) classes
48   (mīsochrēstotatos). But I have been at war at all times with those who think
there could be no good democracy until the slaves and the sort of men who
would sell the city for lack of a drachma (i.e. pay as a Councillor) have a
share in the government; I have also been equally opposed at all times to
these men who think there could be no good oligarchy until the city has fallen
victim to the tyranny of a few men. I, on the other hand, have thought in
the past, and I do not change my opinion now, that it is best to draw up the
constitution in conjunction with those who are able (dunamenoi) to be of service,
49   whether with horses (i.e. as knights) or with shields (i.e. as hoplites). Give one
instance, Critias, if you can, where I have joined with the supporters of either
democracy or tyranny to deprive the 'true gentlemen' (kaloi k'agathoi) of their
citizenship (politeia) . For if I am found guilty of such action, whether now or
in the past, I concede that I deserve to suffer the supreme penalty and be put
to death."

Liturgies

The following speech, delivered in 403/402, illustrates the heavy demand
made on rich citizens, who were nominated in rotation to pay the cost of:-
(a) the maintenance of a trireme for a year, as trierarch;
(b) the production of a chorus at a festival, as chorēgos;
(c) the provision of training-masters in the palaestrae for a year,
     as gymnasiarch;
(d) the provision of a tribal banquet at a festival, as hestiator;
(e) the expenses of a delegation to a foreign festival, as architheōrus;
(f) the maintenance, as a knight, of a horse.
A person nominated could challenge anyone he thought better able to bear
the expense: the latter could then either take over the liturgy or change
properties with his challenger, or appeal to the courts.

Lysias 21. 1-10

1   With regard to the accusations, gentlemen of the jury, you have been sufficiently
guided; but I think you should listen to what remains, too, so that you may know
the character of the person, myself, about whom you are going to vote. I was
approved (dokimasia) as eligible for office in the archonship of Theopompus
(in 411/410) and when appointed chorēgos for the tragic contests, I spent thirty
minae and two months later at the Thargēlia won a victory in the men's chorus
at a cost of two thousand drachmae, and in the archonship of Glaucippus (410/409)
spent eight hundred drachmae upon Pyrrhic dancers at the Great Panathenaea.
2   Furthermore I produced a victorious men's chorus at the Dionysia in the same
archonship, spending five thousand drachmae, including the cost of the dedication

of the tripod; and in the archonship of Diocles (409/408) I spent three hundred
at the Little Panathenaea upon a chorus in the Dithyrambic dance.   Meanwhile
I served as a trierarch for seven years, spending six talents. And though making
all this expenditure and running risks daily and spending periods abroad on your
behalf, I have still contributed special levies (eisphorai), one of thirty minae
and another of four thousand drachmae.   After returning home in the archonship
of Alexias (405/404), I immediately served as gymnasiarch for the winning team
of athletes at the Promethea, at the cost of twelve minae.   Later I was appointed
choregos for a chorus of boys, spending more than fifteen minae.   In the archonship of Eucleides (404/403) I was choregos and produced a winning chorus for
Cephisodorus at the comic contests, spending sixteen minae, including the cost
of the dedication of the costumes, and at the Little Panathenaea I was choregos
of a chorus of beardless Pyrrhic dancers, spending seven minae.   I have been
victorious in the race for triremes off Sunium, at a cost of fifteen minae.   All
this apart from serving as architheoros and providing for the ceremonial
procession (arrephoria) and so on, for which I have spent more than thirty minae.
And I would not have spent even a quarter of the sums I have listed, had I been
willing to confine my liturgies to the specific demands of the law.   During the
period of my trierarchy my ship was the best afloat in the whole fleet.   I shall
quote to you a convincing proof of this.   In the first place Alcibiades, whom I
would have paid a high price to prevent sailing with me, regularly went to sea
on my ship, though he was neither a friend nor relative nor fellow-tribesman
of mine.   Yet I imagine you know that in his office of General he was able to
do what he liked, and he would never have boarded any ship but that with the
best performance, when he was faced with personal danger.   Then after you
deposed Alcibiades and his friends from office (in 406), and elected Thrasyllus
and nine others, all these wanted to go to sea on my ship, but the man to go on
board,   after much argument among them, was Archestratus from Phrearrhe,
and after his death at Mytilene Erasinides sailed with me.   Yet how much money
do you think it cost for a trireme equipped in that way?   How much harm do
you imagine it did to the enemy?   How much good to our city?   Convincing
proof is afforded by the fact that when the fleet was destroyed in the final sea-
battle (at Aegospotami in 405), though no General was sailing with me - a point
I mention since you were angry with the trierarchs too because of the disaster
which had occurred - I both brought my own ship home and rescued that of
Nausimachus from Phaleron. And this was no mere accident, but resulted from
my organisation; for by paying good wages throughout the period I kept as
helmsman Phantias, reputed to be the best in Greece, and I provided the crew
and the rest of the rowers of a quality to match him.   All of you who happened
to be among the troops on that campaign know that I am speaking the truth in
this.   But call Nausimachus as witness.

An account of the duties of a choregos is given by Antiphon in his speech
'On the Choreutes' delivered c.412. An unknown defendant is charged with the
murder of a chorus-boy called Diodotus.

Antiphon, On the Choreutes 11-14

After I was appointed choregos at the Thargelia and was allotted Pantacles
as producer (didaskalos) and the Cecropid tribe to join my own, I carried out
my duties as choregos as efficiently and as fairly as I could.   Firstly, I
equipped a practice-room in the most convenient part of my own house, the
same one in which I produced when I was choregos at the Dionysia.   Next I
assembled the chorus as well as I could, without fining anyone or forcibly
collecting pledges or incurring anyone's enmity, but in the manner that would
prove most agreeable and advantageous to both parties, I issued requests or
invitations, while the parents were ready and willing to send their sons.   When
the boys arrived, at first I did not have time to attend and supervise, since I
happened to have cases pending against Aristion and Philinus, which I considered
it was important, after the impeachment (eisangelia), to prove properly and
correctly before the Council and the rest of the Athenians.   So I was concentrating

on this, but I appointed to manage anything the chorus needed one Phanostratus, a fellow-demesman of the prosecutors here, and a relation of mine by marriage,

13 my son-in-law, and I urged him to do this as carefully as possible. Besides him I appointed two men, Ameinias of the Erechtheid tribe, whom his very tribesmen voted should regularly assemble and supervise the tribe, a man thought to be respectable (chrēstos), and another man. (I also appointed a third man).... of the Cecropid tribe, who regularly used to assemble this tribe. There was also a fourth, Philippus, who had received instructions to buy and spend anything stated by the producer or any of these others, in order that the boys might have their chorus produced as well as possible and

14 lack nothing because of my own preoccupation. That is how my duties as chorēgos proceeded. If I am lying in any of these details to excuse myself, the prosecutor may refute me on any point he likes in his later speech. For this is the situation, gentlemen; many of the spectators here know all the details perfectly, and can hear the officer administering the oath, and are concentrating on my reply to the charge, and I would like both to be thought by them to be keeping my oath myself and by speaking the truth to persuade you to acquit me.

An Athenian Civil Servant

Nicomachus so prolonged his appointment under Thēramenes in 411 as transcriber of the laws that it was not until 399 that he was brought to court for refusing to give an account of his public duties in the normal way.

Lysias 30. 1-8, 9-14

1 It has sometimes happened, gentlemen of the jury, that men brought to trial have been thought guilty, but on demonstrating the merits (aretai) of their ancestors and their own good services have obtained pardon at your hands. So since you accept it from defendants if it is demonstrable that they have done the state some service, it is right that you should also listen to prosecutors if they demonstrate that the accused have long been villains (ponēroi)

2 Well, it would be laborious to describe how Nicomachus' father was a public slave, what Nicomachus' youthful career was like, at what age he was introduced to his official brotherhood (phratry), but everyone knows how he defiled the city after he became a transcriber (anagrapheus) of the laws: after receiving a commission to transcribe the laws of Solon within four months, he made himself law-giver (nomothetēs) in Solon's place and stretched the office over six years instead of

3 four months, and for a daily fee he included or erased laws. We reached such a condition that we had the laws doled out to us from his hands, and rivals in the jury-courts quoted contradictory laws, both claiming to have received them from Nicomachus. Though the archons imposed summary fines and brought him to court, he refused to hand the laws over, but the city met with the severest disasters before he was relieved of his office and faced audit (euthūnai) for his

4 activities. Let me point out, gentlemen of the jury, that after avoiding punishment for all that, he has now treated his office in the same way. In the first place he transcribed laws for four years, when he might have been quit of the task within thirty days; second, although it had been defined from what sources the transcription was to be made, he gave himself general authority, and unprecedentedly he alone of office-holders has failed to submit to euthūnai for his

5 management. While everyone else renders account of his office in each prytany, you, Nicomachus, did not even deign to submit a record in four years, but you imagine that you alone of citizens are licensed to hold office for a long time, without submitting to euthūnai or obeying the decrees (psēphismata) or heeding the laws, but you include this, erase that, and have reached such a pitch of arrogance (hubris) that you imagine the city's property belongs to yourself,

6 though you yourself are a public servant. So, gentlemen of the jury, you should remember who Nicomachus' ancestors were, and as Nicomachus has treated you ungratefully by his breaches of the law, you should punish him, and as you have not inflicted punishment for each individual act, so now at least exact retribution for them all.

7   But perhaps, gentlemen of the jury, when he is unable to offer any defence of himself, he will endeavour to slander me. But I think you should believe him about my career only if I am unable to prove him a liar when I am granted right of reply. If in fact he attempts to say what he did in the Council, that I was one of the Four Hundred, bear in mind that on the basis of such statements there will be more than a thousand in the Four Hundred; for those who wish to slander those who were still children at that time or abroad , use this insult.

8   I was so far from being a member of the Four Hundred that I was not even included in the list of the Five Thousand. . . . .

9   I regard it as also remarkable that Nīcomachus thinks it right to show unjust malice towards others, when he is a man whom I shall prove to have plotted against the plēthos. Now listen to me, gentlemen of the jury; it is right to admit such accusations when dealing with the sort of men who then joined in

10   overthrowing the dēmos but now claim to be democrats. For when the revolution was being organised after the destruction of the fleet, Cleophon repeatedly abused the Council, saying it was in conspiracy and not deliberating in the city's best interests. Satyrus from Cēphisia, a Councillor, persuaded

11   the Council to arrest Nīchomachus and bring him to court. Those who wanted to destroy him, afraid that they might fail to gain a death penalty in the jury-court, persuaded Nīcomachus to publish a law that the Council too should join in the trial as fellow-jurymen. And this utter villain (ponēros) was so obviously an accomplice in the plot that on the day when the trial took place he published

12   the law. Now one might bring other charges against Cleophon, gentlemen of the jury; but this is universally agreed, that those who overthrew the democracy wanted him out of the way above all citizens, and that Satyrus and Chremon, the members of the Thirty, did not accuse Cleophon in rage on your behalf, but

13   so that after executing him they themselves might injure you. This they achieved because of the law which Nīcomachus published. So, gentlemen of the jury, it is reasonable that even those of you who thought Cleophon was a bad citizen should reflect that perhaps there were villains (ponēroi) among those who were executed during the oligarchy; but even so you were enraged with the Thirty because of these men too, because they did not execute them on account

14   of their crimes but under pressure of stasis . Therefore if he defends himself on this charge, remember this, that he published the law at the very time at which revolution was taking place, and as a favour to these destroyers of democracy, and caused the Council, in which Satyrus and Chremon were most influential (dunatoi), to join in the trial as fellow-jurymen, while Strombichides, Calliades and many other true gentlemen (kaloi k'agathoi) among the citizens were put to death.

The Bitterness of Politics at Athens

    Plato tells the story of his experiences in Athens when ordered government collapsed under the stress of external defeat and civil strife within. Cf. Thucydides, 3. 82. 2 - 83 (P. 2C8-211), for an account of stasis at Corcyra.

Plato, Seventh Letter, 324 B - 325 C   (written after 353)

324 B   As a young man I had the same experience as very many others. I had intended
    C   as soon as I was my own master to go straight into politics. Then I happened to be influenced by political events in Athens; the regime (politeia) of the time had been widely unpopular, and the turn of events led to a revolution (in 404). The leaders of this revolution were fifty-one men, consisting of eleven in Athens and ten in the Piraeus to look after the Agora and other local duties in the two cities, and thirty with plenipotentiary powers (autokratores) to control the general
    D   situation. Now some of these men happened to be members of my family and well-known to me, and indeed they asked me to join them as if it was, so to speak, a family affair. Young as I was, I did not regard this as anything extraordinary and supposing that their administration would improve the moral tone of the city, I watched eagerly to see what they would do. And, believe me, what I saw them do soon made the previous regime (politeia) seem a

golden age by comparison. To give you one example, they tried to send
Socrates, a friend of mine, getting on in years, and a man I feel justified
in calling the most upright of his time - they tried to send him with others
to fetch a fellow-citizen by force to be put to death, just so that they could
implicate Socrates in their regime whether he wanted or not: and he refused,
risking any form of punishment rather than besmirch himself with their
monstrous activities. This was the sort of thing I saw - and there were
plenty of similar episodes of similar gravity - and so I withdrew in distaste
from the evils of the time. But not long afterwards the whole regime of the
Thirty was overthrown: and slowly but surely the old ambition for politics
began to draw me. Well, the new regime was naturally at sixes and sevens
and much happened that was objectionable: old scores were sometimes
paid to excess, which is not surprising in a time of revolution. All the same,
the exiles who returned at that time showed great moderation (epieikeia). But,
as ill-luck would have it, some of the powerful men of the time (dunasteuontes)
brought a court-case against this same Socrates, our companion, accusing
him monstrously and quite undeservedly of impiety. He was prosecuted,
condemned and put to death, he who, at the time his accusers were themselves
suffering in exile, refused, as I said, to have any part in the monstrous arrest
of one of their fellow-exiles.

E
325 A

B

C

Socrates' Two Encounters with Politics

> Socrates has explained that his Divine Sign has restrained him from
> engaging in politics. It seems clear that Plato is here reconstructing
> Socrates' life on the basis of his own experience of Athenian politics
> (cf. his Seventh Letter, above). For, although we may accept the
> two incidents as genuine, and perhaps even typical of the years of bitter
> civil strife from 411 onwards, they do not apply to the settled conditions
> of the early Periclean period, which is when Socrates would have made
> his decision not to attempt a political career.

Plato, Apology 31 D - 32 E

31 D

E

32 A

B

C

You know well, men of Athens, that, if long ago I had tried to enter politics,
long ago too I should have been killed and have been of no benefit either to
you or to myself. Do not be angry with me for speaking the truth: for it is
true that no man can hope to save his skin who genuinely opposes you or any
other plēthos and constantly tries to prevent contravention of morality and
law. Any true would-be champion of morality must, if he is even for a short
time to save his skin, confine himself to acting as a private citizen and avoiding
public life.
I will give you convincing evidence of what I say, no mere verbal proofs but the
sort of proof you respect - concrete evidence. Let me recount my experiences
that you may know that no man will ever force me through fear of death to act
against what is right but that I would far rather die. My story is brash, lawcourt stuff, but true. The only public office I ever held, men of Athens, was
membership of the Council: and it happened to be in our tribe's prytany that
you decided to try in a body the ten Generals who failed to rescue the men
from the sea after the Battle of Arginusae - an unconstitutional decision,
as you all subsequently agreed. On that occasion I was the only one of the
prytaneis to oppose you and to vote against doing anything contrary to the
laws; and, although the politicians (rhētores) were prepared to bring an
indictment against me and take me summarily to court, and although you were
loud-voiced in urging them to do so, I saw it as my duty to take the side of law
and justice and risk the consequences rather than go along with you in your
unjust proposal through fear of prison or death. This took place when Athens
was still a democracy. When the oligarchy took over, there was another
similar episode. The Thirty sent for me with four others to come to the Tholos

and ordered us to fetch from Salamis Leon, the Salaminian, so that they could
put him to death - an order typical of many of their orders, intent as they were
on implicating as many people as possible in the guilt of their actions.   Well,
then again I showed, not in word but in deed, that, to put it crudely, death means

D nothing to me, but the avoidance of committing an offence against justice or
morality - that means everything to me.   The government of the time, powerful
as it was, could not cow me into an act of injustice, but when we left the Tholos,
the other four went off to Salamis and fetched Leon, but I went off home.   And I
might very well have been put to death for this, had not the Thirty soon fallen.

E Of the truth of my story many people will bear witness.

A Plea for Moderation in 405

Aristophanes, Frogs 686-705

It is right for our sacred chorus to give good (chrēstos) advice and instruction
to the city.   First we think that all the citizens should be put on a par and that
all fear should be removed;   and if any have been thrown by Phrynichus' tricks,

690 then I declare that they must be granted a chance to shed the blame for past
slips and make up for their former mistakes.   Secondly, I say that no citizen
should be disfranchised (atīmos).   For it is a disgrace that while those who
fought in one sea-battle should, like the Plataeans, immediately become masters

695 instead of slaves, - not that I would say this was wrong;   indeed I approve of it.
This was your only sensible action.   But besides this, it is reasonable that at
their constant request you should forgive for this one misfortune those who are

700 your kin and have fought on your side many times, as did their fathers.   Your
wisdom (sophia) is instinctive, so let us abate our anger and willingly take as
our kin and as fully enfranchised (epitīmoi) citizens every man who fights in
the navy with us.   But if we swell with arrogant pride like this, especially when

705 our city is in the clutches of the waves, in later times our policies will appear
foolish.

In 406/405 Athens had issued bronze coins in place of the normal gold
or silver for the first time.   Aristophanes likens the admission of an
alien riff-raff to the magistracies, when Athenians of pure blood were
excluded, to the introduction of this debased coinage.

Aristophanes, Frogs 718-737

We have often thought that the city's treatment of the true gentlemen (kaloi

720 k'agathoi) among her citizens was the same as her use of the old currency
and the recent gold coins.   We make no use of those coins, which are not
adulterated, but which are in my opinion the finest of all anywhere in Greece
or abroad, the only ones to have been properly struck and soundly tested.

725 Instead we use this common (ponēros) bronze coinage of a very bad stamp,
struck but a day or two ago.   Likewise we maltreat those citizens we
recognise to be noble (eugeneis), sensible (sōphrones), just, and true
gentlemen (kaloi k'agathoi), who were educated in wrestling, dancing and

730 music (mousikē).   The men we employ for everything are like the debased
bronze coinage - foreigners, red-heads, commoners (ponēroi) who are the
sons of commoners, the most recent arrivals in Athens, all men whom the city
would not readily have employed before, even as scapegoats.   But now, you

735 fools, change your ways;   respect once more respectable (chrēstoi) citizens.   If
you meet with success, the credit will be yours;   if not, the wise will think,
if you do suffer any reverse, that at least you were hanged from a decent tree.

The Folly of the Politicians

This extract from the speech 'On the Peace', written in 355, contains
a half-truth about the fifth century.   Its generalizations about the
decline of Athens are typical of Isocrates' attitude to history.

Isocrates, On the Peace 75-86; 88-89

75 Now the superiority in quality and strength of the government (politeia) of that time over the one which was later established was equal to that of such fine men as Aristides and Themistocles and Miltiades compared to Hyperbolus and Cleophon and our present demagogues. But the dēmos which governed at that period you will find was not full of idleness, indecision, or empty hopes,

76 but was able to defeat in battles all who invaded the country, and was adjudged worthy of prizes for valour in perils faced on behalf of Greece, and inspired such trust that the majority of the states voluntarily placed themselves in their

77 hands. Despite these advantages, this power encouraged us to a degree of irresponsibility (akolasia) such as no man could approve of, instead of the system of government (politeia) which was universally esteemed. And instead of our

78 defeating those who marched against us, it trained the citizens in such a way that they did not even dare to go out to meet the enemy in front of the walls, while in place of the goodwill towards them on the part of the allies and the reputation which they enjoyed in the rest of Greece, it caused them to be so detested that the state came within an inch of being enslaved, and would have been so, had we not found the Spartans, who originally waged war on us, more

79 generous than those who were formerly our allies. We would have no right to criticise them for being rendered ill-disposed towards us, for this sort of policy towards us was not fundamental, but adopted in retaliation for many dreadful experiences. Who could have endured the effrontery of our fathers, who assembled from all over Greece, the idlest folk and those involved in all manner of villainies (ponēriai), manning their triremes with these, and thus incurred the hatred of the Greeks, and exiled the best (beltistoi) citizens in the other cities, while distributing their possessions to the most villainous (poneroi)

80 Greeks? But assuredly, were I to dare to describe in detail what happened during that period, I might perhaps cause you to adopt better plans about the present situation, but would myself be slandered; for you usually detest not

81 so much those responsible for mistakes as those who prosecute them. So because of this attitude of yours I am afraid that I may myself reap some insult while trying to benefit you. I shall not indeed entirely abandon what I had in mind, but shall pass over the most offensive items which would most hurt your feelings, and mention only this point, from which you will recognise the folly of the

82 politicians of that time. So precise were they in discovering the means by which men might incur most hatred that they passed a decree (psēphisma) to divide up the surplus of the revenues, a talent at a time, and bring it into the dancing-area (orchēstra) at the (Great) Dionysia, when the theatre was full: they did this, and they also brought in the sons of those who had died in the war, making a display to both groups, showing the allies the value of their capital investment being brought in by paid men, and showing the other Greeks the number of orphans and

83 the disasters which befell them because of this aggressive policy. As they did this they themselves congratulated their city on its luck, and many of the unintelligent counted it fortunate, lacking any foresight of what was likely to happen because of this, but envying and marvelling at the wealth, which had entered their city unjustly and was likely soon to destroy also that prosperity which had justly been

84 theirs. For so far did they come to disregard their own property and covet that of others that, even when the Spartans had invaded their country and the fort at Decelea had been established, they manned triremes to sail against Sicily, and they were not ashamed to let their own country be ravaged and pillaged,

85 and yet send out an army against those who had never done us any harm; they reached such a depth of stupidity that, although they did not control their own suburbs, they expected to conquer Italy, Sicily, and Carthage. They so excelled all mankind in folly that, while disasters brace up other men and render them

86 more sensible, they did not even learn lessons from them. Yet they encountered more numerous and more severe disasters during this period of government than those which had ever befallen the city before ......

88 Finally they failed to realise that they had filled the public graves with their citizens, and the official brotherhoods (phratries) and the census registers

with people having nothing to do with the state. From these in particular
one can ascertain the number of casualties; for the families of those of highest
renown and the grandest houses, who had escaped both the political purges
(staseis) under the tyrants and the Persian war, we shall find during the period
89   of empire which we yearn after, were uprooted. So, should one desire to make
a general reflection, referring to this as an indicator, it might almost appear
that we were a new people.

19.   THE ATHENIAN CHARACTER AFTER THE WAR

Extreme Democracy

> Although the dramatic date of the Republic is perhaps as early as 424,
> Plato is here drawing on his experience of developments up to c.390.
> The modern reader will perhaps not accept so unquestioningly the analogy
> between the democratic man and the democratic state, although comparison
> of individual and state is a common procedure in this part of the Republic.

Plato, Republic 557 A - 558 C

557 A   Democracy, I think, comes into being when the poor defeat the rich and either put
them to death or banish them, and then share out equally among those left in the
city all political privilege (politeia) and offices, most offices being conferred
by lot.
Yes, he said, that is how democracy comes about, whether it is established by
force of arms or the rich simply slip away in fright.
What then is their way of life, I said, and what form of constitution is involved?
B   Obviously a man organized on the same lines will emerge as our democratic
man.
Obviously.
Well, their first characteristic is freedom. The city is brimfull of freedom
of action (eleutheria) and of speech (parrhēsia). A man may do as he likes in
it. Isn't that so?
So they say.
And where there is this general permissiveness (exousia), every individual will
of course arrange his own life as he pleases.
Of course.
C   And I think this constitution more than any other will be remarkable for the
varied character of its inhabitants.
True enough.
Perhaps, I said, it is the most attractive of all the constitutions. Like a many-
coloured garment decorated with dyes of every shade, democracy is decorated
with every sort of characteristic, and people are attracted in much the same way
as women and children love looking at many-coloured things: and so perhaps
many will find democracy the most beautiful constitution.
They will indeed.
D   And what's more, my dear fellow, I said, a democracy is a very convenient spot
to look for a constitution.
Why?
Because it contains every kind of constitution thanks to its permissiveness (exousia);
and anyone who, like ourselves a short while ago, wanted to draw up a blue-print
for a city would be bound to find that he could go to a democratically ruled city and
pick out whatever way of doing things he liked best, as if from some supermarket
of constitutions, and use it for his purpose.
E   Well, I agree he would probably have plenty of patterns to choose from at any
rate.
And just think, I said: in this city no one need govern, even if capable of doing
so, nor on the other hand need anyone be governed if he does not so choose; you
need not fight when the rest fight, nor keep the peace when the rest do, unless
peace is what you want; and, again, if some law debars you from holding office
558 A   or sitting on a jury, you can none the less do so, if you yourself feel inclined.
Isn't that a wonderfully attractive way of life for the moment?

For the moment perhaps it is.

Then there's their delightful leniency (praotēs) sometimes towards condemned men. You must have noticed how in a democracy men who have been sentenced to death or exile often none the less remain at large in the city, and you'll see one of them loafing around without anyone's paying any heed or seeing him any more than if he were a spirit returned to earth.

Yes, I have often seen such men.

B   Then there is the generally considerate attitude and the absolute refusal to be pedantic, and the scorn for the precepts we spoke of with reverence when we were designing our city and we said that, short of being blessed with an exceptional nature, a man could never become good, unless right from childhood he played in lovely surroundings and practised in every way lovely habits. All this our democracy tramples in lordly manner under foot and cares not at
C   all what moral training a man has had for entering politics. All he has to say to win approval is that he is on the side of the plēthos.

Yes, he said, it is a very grand attitude.

Well, I said, these and the like are the characteristics of democracy and I think we may sum it up as a constitution which is attractive and anarchic and various, one which distributes equality alike to the equal and the unequal.

There are no surprises in that definition.

Plato on the Democratic Man

It has often been pointed out that Plato must have had Alcibiades in mind for parts of this passage.

Plato, Republic 559 D - 562 A

559 D   Very well, I said, let us now in turn describe how the democratic man arises out of the oligarchic man. I think it usually happens in the following way. A young man, brought up, as we have just described, without true education (apaideutos) and in a niggardly spirit, gets a taste of the drones' honey and joins a wild and terrible gang of them who can provide him with delights of every sort and shade and shape. It is somewhere here you must look for
E   the seeds of the change from the oligarchic to the democratic within him.

I agree absolutely, he said.

And I suggest that just as our city began to change when one faction received help from outside allies, like helping like, so too our young man begins to change when one of the sides to his nature receives outside help from a brand of desires which is congenial and similar.

Undoubtedly.

And if, I imagine, some counter-alliance rallies to the support of the oligarchic side of his nature, coming perhaps from his father or from the admonitions and
560 A   rebukes of his other relatives, then there arises in him faction (stasis) and counter-faction (antistasis) and a battle in himself against himself. At first the democratic part in him may yield to the oligarchic part and some of his desires may be either destroyed or banished, as a sort of shame is created in the young man's soul, and order is restored within him.

Sometimes this happens, he said.

But then, I imagine, other desires of the same breed as the banished desires
B   are nurtured in secret and, thanks to the father's ignorance of how to bring his son up, they become numerous and powerful.

That at any rate is what often happens.

And so these desires draw him towards the same old companionships and, breeding secretly together, produce a huge brood (plēthos).

And then?

Then finally they seize the citadel (acropolis) of the young man's soul, perceiving that it is empty of the troops of learning and noble training and true reason, which are, to be sure, the best guardians and custodians in the minds of men who are loved by the gods.

C   They certainly are, he said.

And in their place rushes up an occupation army of lying and braggart theories
and opinions.

Yes, Indeed.

Then, surely, the young man returns to his old **Lotus**-eater friends and openly
lives with them; and if a relieving force from his relatives comes to the help
of the thrifty part of his soul, the army of braggart theories shuts the gates of
the royal wall within him and will neither admit the relieving force nor listen

D   to the ambassadorial words of individual elders, but themselves take control
by force: decency they dub folly and thrust unceremoniously into exile; restraint
(sōphrosynē) they call cowardice and banish with a hail of abuse; moderation
and modest expenditure they represent as peasant vulgarity and meanness and
send them over the border with the help of a crowd of useless desires.

They do indeed.

Of all these qualities they empty and cleanse the soul of the young man under

E   their sway, - their initiate in a grandiose ceremony. And now the stage is set
to usher in violence (hubris) and anarchy and profligacy and shamelessness,
glorified by a large attendant rout and by garlands on their heads, and to the
accompaniment of panegyrics and euphemistic endearments, - violence (hubris)
being called 'good education' (eupaideusia), anarchy 'freedom', profligacy

561 A   'magnificence' and shamelessness 'courage'. Such, more or less, must be
the state of the young man when he changes from the man who was brought up
on a regime of essential desires and adopts the free and easy regime of inessential
and useless pleasures.

That is quite clearly so, he said.

And thereafter, I imagine, the life of our young man is devoted indiscriminately
to essential and inessential pleasures alike, and he squanders his money and his
efforts and his time on both. If he is lucky and not utterly crazed by the rite
he has undergone, he may, when he is older and the tumult and the shouting has

B   died, allow back some of the exiles and not surrender entirely to the invaders.
In this case he will lead a life based on an equilibrium of the pleasures, indifferently
surrendering, as it were, the government of his soul now to this pleasure, now
to that, on the lottery principle, until he is sated, debarring none of them but
fostering all alike.

Agreed.

And since, I went on, he will not listen to nor admit to the stronghold any true
reasoning, if someone says that some pleasures come from noble and good

C   (kalos te kai agathos) desires and should be practised and honoured, whereas
others come from wicked (ponēros) desires and should be disciplined and subjected,
then he just disagrees and says that all pleasures are alike and equally to be
honoured.

That is very much his disposition and behaviour.

His daily habits too reflect this gratification of the whim of the moment. At
one moment he is besotted with wine and the flute, at the next he is off alcohol

D   and on a diet; now he is in **training**, now he is idle and utterly uninterested,
now he acts the philosopher. Often he takes part in politics and jumping to
his feet says and does whatever occurs to him; and if the military take his
fancy, he's off to join them - and next it's the business-men. And there's no
order or principle about his life, but calling it 'the pleasant life' and 'the free
life' and 'the happy life' he lives it all the time.

E   You have certainly given a full description, he said, of what one may call 'the
egalitarian man' (isonomikos).

I may add perhaps, I said, that he is a man of all sorts and brim-full of different
characteristics: he is in fact the attractive and many-coloured man corresponding
to the city we described: and many men and women may well envy him his life,
possessing as he does the largest number of patterns whether for constitutions
or individual characters.

You have identified the man, he said.

562 A   Shall we then agree that this is the sort of man who can properly be called the
democratic man and be set alongside the democratic state?

Agreed.

Plato on the Breakdown of Status in a Democracy

Plato, Republic 562 B - 563 E

562 B I suggest that democracy too, just like the other constitutions, is destroyed by an excessive realization of its own particular ideal.
Which is?

C Freedom, I said. I am sure you must agree that in a democracy you will hear people saying that freedom is its finest feature and what makes it the only state worth living in for a man born to be free.
Yes, one often hears that said.
Well, I was going to say that it is the excess of freedom and the neglect of other things which make even this constitution change and make it ripe for tyranny.
How? he said.
When a democracy in its thirst for freedom falls under the charge of bad wine-

D waiters (oinochooi prostatountes) and is given wine undiluted and gets excessively drunk, then, I think, unless its so-called rulers are very lenient (praoi) and allow abundant freedom, it punishes them for being 'damned oligarchs'.
True.
And those who obey their rulers are slanged as 'willing slaves' and 'nobodies'.
In fact both in public and in private life praise and honour go to the man who, if a ruler, behaves like a subject and, if a subject, behaves like a ruler. In

E this sort of constitution the ideal of 'freedom' is bound to go to extremes. And it will even, my friend, find its way into private households and finally breed anarchy among the animals.
Just explain that bit of our story.
The sort of thing I mean, I said, is that a father is conditioned to swapping status with his sons and being frightened of them - instead of they of him : correspondingly the son learns to feel no respect for or fear of his parents -

563 A all in the cause of freedom. And, there is a similar levelling process between citizen and metic, and citizen and foreigner.
Yes, this does happen.
I can give you a few other little examples. In this sort of climate the teacher begins to fear his pupils and curry favour with them, and the pupils begin to despise their teachers and their tutors too. And in general the young assume the mantle of their elders and vie with them in word and deed, while the old

B come down to the level of the young and, in their effort to imitate them, breathe adaptability and humour, to avoid the unthinkable charge of being 'kill-joys', or 'dictators' (despotikoi).
True enough.
And the furthest stage of the glut of freedom in this sort of city is when slaves, male and female, from the slave-market are just as free as their purchasers.
Oh! and I nearly forgot to mention the equality of status (isonomia) and the freedom engendered between men and women.

C Shall we then as Aeschylus says, 'utter what just sprang to our lips'?
Certainly, I said. I am uttering my thoughts as they come to me spontaneously.
My remark about the comparative freedom of domestic animals in a democracy must seem incredible to anyone who has not witnessed it. The fact is that the old proverb 'like mistress, like dog' becomes literally true - and not only of dogs. Horses and donkeys arise, accustomed to walk along in free and haughty fashion, bumping into anyone who crosses their path in the streets if he doesn't

D get out of their way. It's freedom, freedom everywhere.
You are 'telling me my own dream' he said. I have often had just this experience on my way to the country.
In short, I said, if you take all this into account, you can see how soft it all makes the character of the citizens, so that they reject and will not tolerate the smallest degree of slavery anyone may require of them. And I imagine you realise that eventually they do not heed even the laws, written or unwritten,

E just to ensure that they shall never in any way have a master.
I realise that well enough.

Plato on the Three Elements in a Democracy

Plato, Republic 564 C – 565 D

564 C   Very well, I said, to get a clearer view of our problem, let us divide our notional democracy into the three elements which in fact characterize actual democracies.

D   One element, you'll agree, is the drone-element which, thanks to the permissiveness (exousia), thrives just as much in a democracy as in an oligarchy.
Yes.
But in a democracy this element is much more militant. In an oligarchy it is without privilege (not entimos) and is kept away from office, and so becomes out of condition and enfeebled; but in a democracy it is this element, I suggest, which, with a few exceptions, takes the lead in the government. The most militant among them make the speeches and take the actions, while the rest

E   settle round the speakers' platforms and buzz down any opposition speaker. Yes, practically everything in a democracy is run by the drone-element.
It is indeed, he said.
Then there is always a second element which becomes distinct from the plethos. Where everyone is engaged in trying to make money, I suppose it is those with the most inborn good-sense who usually become the wealthiest?
Probably.
It is from them, I think, that the drones get their most abundant and easy supply of honey.
Well, one could scarcely get honey from the poor.
This element, then, the drone-fodder, is generally styled 'the rich'.
Usually.

565 A   And the demos form the third element – I mean those who work their own land and are not politically active (apragmones), men without much capital. This indeed is the largest and most powerful element in a democracy, if once it is concentrated.
Yes, he said, but usually it won't concentrate, unless it gets a taste of the honey.
And this taste is regulated by the leaders on the principle 'soak the capitalists, distribute the proceeds to the demos, but keep the bulk yourself'.

B   That's the principle.
And the rich who are soaked inevitably react by making speeches in the Assembly of the demos and taking whatever other steps they can to protect themselves.
Naturally.
Thus, even if in fact they have no desire for revolution (neoterizein), they are accused by the drone-element of plotting against the demos and favouring

C   oligarchy. And eventually when they see the demos – not willingly but out of ignorance, gulled as they are by the authors of the slander – treating them unjustly, then they do, willy-nilly, become real oligarchs, not of their own accord but stung to it by our infamous drone who thus adds another to the evils he has engendered.
Very true.
And so arise impeachments (eisangeliai) and condemnations and court-cases between the two sides.
Yes.
And the demos is apt to choose one particular person as their champion (prostates) and to nurse him and build him up.
Yes.

D   One thing seems clear then – it is in this championship of the people and nowhere else that we must look for the root of the subsequent emergence of a tyrant.

Pay for the Assembly

Early in the fourth century the political situation at Athens was so changed that pay had been introduced to counteract the low attendance at the Assembly. Cf. Aristotle, Constitution of Athens 41.3:- 'Agyrrhius first introduced a fee of one obol; after him, Heracleides of Clazomenae, with the surname 'king' made it two obols, and then again Agyrrhius (not later than 392) increased it to three obols.'

Aristophanes, Ecclesiazusae 289-310 (produced probably in 392)

290 Let us proceed to the Assembly, gentlemen. For the thesmothetes has threatened that anyone who fails to arrive at dawn, covered in dust, exuding contentment from his garlic-pickle breakfast, and looking like vinegar, shall not get his three obols. Now then, Charitimides, Smikythos, and Drakes, hurry up and
295 follow me, and be careful not to strike a wrong note and give yourself away. Let us get our token (symbolon) and then sit together, so that we can pass all the measures our dear sisters want. Oh dear, what am I talking about? 'Brothers' is the name I ought to have given them.

300 Let us be sure to push aside these men who have come from the town. Before, when they received only one obol for their attendance, they would sit around gossiping among the flower-stalls, but nowadays they're too much like a rabble (ochlos) here. In the days when noble (gennadas) Myronides held office
305 (c. 457), no one would have ventured to take money for joining in the administration of the state. Each man attended, bringing his drink in a little goatskin, as well as a loaf for himself, two onions, and three olives. But nowadays, just like a
310 gang of navvies, their main concern is to get their three obols whenever they do a job for the community.

INDEX

The following numbers refer to pages of this volume: except that in the case of Thucydides (Thuc.) they refer to the page-numbers of the Penguin translation of Thucydides, and in the case of the Old Oligarch (O.O.) to the sections of that work, which may be looked up in LACTOR 2, The Old Oligarch. Important references are underlined.

imperialism, 25f., 56; Thuc. 129ff., 180ff., 379; O.O. I, 14-II, 6
imports, 10; Thuc. 118; O.O. II, 7
isonomia, 1, 2, 60; Thuc. 117, 210, 377, 392

jurymen (dicasts), 7, 8, 16, 22, 23f., 25f.; O.O. I, 13, 16, 18, III, 6-7

kaloi k'agathoi, 11, 15, 44, 50, 53, 55; cf. 59
Knights (cavalry - hippeis), 7, 17, 21, 38, 44, 45; cf. 50 and Thuc. 527

lawcourts, 24; O.O. I, 13, 16, 18; III, 6-7; see also jurymen.
laws, attitude to, 6, 14, 29, 32ff., 41, 48, 52f., 54; Thuc. 117, 126f.,
    181, 209ff., 376; O.O. I, 5, 8-9
litigation, love of, 23ff., 44
liturgies, 40, 50ff.; Thuc. 377; cf. 106; O.O. I, 13, III, 4
lot, 2, 4, 8, 57; cf. 9; O.O. I, 2-3

middle classes, 3; cf. 50; Thuc. 210, 547
morals, 32ff., 53, 54, 58; Thuc. 126f., 208ff.

naval populace, 20, 51, 56; Thuc. 385, 529f.; O.O. I, 2, 19-20
Nicias, 8, 13ff.; Thuc. 246f., 372ff.

oligarchy, 2; cf. 4, 61; Thuc. 392; cf. O.O. I, 5; see also Four Hundred.
ostracism, 8, 9; Thuc. 529

parties, political, 7, 8, 11; Thuc. 209ff.
pay, 4, 7, 8, 11, 15, 18ff., 24, 25, 26, 40, 62; Thuc. 382, 385, 547;
    O.O. I, 3
Peisander, 37, 41, 49; Thuc. 516, 518f., 523ff.
Pericles, 8, 11f., 13ff., 22, 30; Thuc. esp. 117ff., 134f.
Pericles, the Younger, 44, 46ff.; cf. 30
Phrynichus, 42, 43, 55; Thuc. 516ff., 526
polypragmosynē, 11, 27f.; O.O. II, 18
prostatēs (tou dēmou), 2, 3, 7, 13, 17, 27, 39, 46, 60, 61; Thuc. 135
prytaneis, 8ff., 17f., 20, 21, 30, 35, 38, 40, 47, 54
psēphismata, 6, 37, 40, 42, 47f., 52, 56
public buildings, 11-12; O.O. II, 9-10

revenue, 25f.; O.O. I, 16-18
rhētores, 13, 16, 18, 20, 23, 54, 61; Thuc. 384, 489
rich and poor, 2, 3, 4, 23, 57, 61; Thuc. 118, 120, 134; O.O. I, 2, 4, 13-14
rural populace, 2f., 4f., 18, 23, 43, 61; Thuc. 106ff., 448; O.O. II, 14

slaves, 37, 55, 60; Thuc. 180, 448; O.O. I, 10-12
Socrates, 31ff., 44, 47, 54f.
Solon, 27, 40
sophists, 28, 29f., 31; Thuc. 182
sōphrosynē, 11, 28, 29, 44, 55, 59
stasis, 2, 7, 8, 11, 40, 53ff., 57; Thuc. 208ff.
stratēgoi - see Generals
sycophants, 9, 27f., 43

Thēramenes, 13f., 41, 46ff., 49, 50; Thuc. 526
thesmothetai, 42, 62
Thirty, the, 46, 50, 53, 54f.
tribes, 6f.
tribute, 7f., 11-12, 22, 25f.; cf. Thuc. 449; O.O. III, 2, 5
tyranny, 1ff., 35; cf. 61; Thuc. 399ff.

young and old, 28f., 31, 58f., 60; Thuc. 375, 379